Robert Hall, John Clayton

Christianity

Robert Hall, John Clayton

Christianity

ISBN/EAN: 9783744660914

Printed in Europe, USA, Canada, Australia, Japan

Cover: Foto ©Lupo / pixelio.de

More available books at **www.hansebooks.com**

ANSWER

TO

MR. CLAYTON's SERMON.

[Price One Shilling and Six-pence.]

CHRISTIANITY

CONSISTENT WITH A

LOVE OF FREEDOM:

BEING AN

ANSWER

TO A

SERMON,

LATELY PUBLISHED

BY THE REV. JOHN CLAYTON.

BY ROBERT HALL, M.A.

LONDON:
PRINTED FOR J. JOHNSON, (N° 72,) ST. PAUL'S
CHURCH-YARD, 1791.

PREFACE.

IT may be proper juſt to remark, that the animadverſions I have made on Mr. Clayton's Sermon did not ariſe from my conviction of there being any thing even of plauſibility in his reaſonings, but from an apprehenſion, that certain accidental and occaſional prejudices might give ſome degree of weight to one of the weakeſt defences of a bad cauſe that was ever undertaken. I have taken up more time in ſhowing that there is no *proper connexion* between the Unitarian doctrine and the principles of liberty than the ſubject may ſeem to require ; but this will not be thought ſuperfluous by thoſe who recollect that that idea ſeems to be the great hinge

PREFACE.

hinge of Mr. Clayton's difcourfe, and that it appears amongft the orthodox part of the Diffenters to have been productive already of unhappy effects. I fhall only add, that thefe remarks would have appeared much fooner but for fevere indifpofition, and that I was induced to write them chiefly from a perfuafion that they might perhaps, in the prefent inftance, have fomewhat of additional weight as coming from one who is *not* an Unitarian.

Cambridge,
Sept. 17, 1791.

# CONTENTS.

SECTION I.
On the duty of private Chriſtians in relation to civil polity. 5

SECTION II.
On the duty of Miniſters in relation to civil government. 22

SECTION III.
On the pretences Mr. Clayton advances for his doctrines. 42

SECTION IV.
On the Teſt Act. 63

CHRISTIANITY,

CONSISTENT WITH A

LOVE OF FREEDOM, &c.

THIS is a period diftinguifhed for extraordinary occurrences, whether we contemplate the world under its larger divifions, or in refpect to thofe fmaller communities and parties, into which it is broken and divided. We have lately witneffed, with aftonifhment and regret, the attempts of a celebrated orator to overthrow the principles of freedom, which he has rendered himself illuftrious by defending; as well as to cover with reproach the characters of thofe by whom, in the earlier part of life, he was moft careffed and diftinguifhed. The fuccefs of thefe efforts is pretty generally known, and is fuch as it might have been expected would have been fufficient to deter from fimilar attempts. But we now behold a diffenting minifter coming forth to the public under the character of a flatterer of power, and an *accufer of his brethren*. If the fplendid eloquence that adorns every part of Mr. Burke's celebrated book cannot fhelter the author from confutation, and his fyftem from contempt, Mr. Clayton, with talents fo far inferior, has but little to expect in the fame caufe. It is not eafy to conceive the motives which could impel him to publifh his fermon. From his own account it fhould feem he was anxious to difabufe the legiflature, and to convince them there are many amongft the diffenters who highly difapprove the fentiments and conduct of the more patriotic part of their brethren.

How

How far he may be qualified from his talents or connexions, as a mouth, to declare the sentiments of any considerable portion of the dissenters, I shall not pretend to decide, but shall candidly confess, there are not wanting amongst us persons who are ready upon all occasions to oppose those principles on which the very existence of our dissent is founded. Every party will have its apostates of this kind; it is our consolation, however, that their numbers are comparatively small; that they are generally considered as our reproach, and that their conduct is in a great measure the effect of necessity, as they consist almost entirely of persons who can only make themselves heard by confusion and discord. If our author wishes to persuade the legislature the friends of arbitrary power are conspicuous for their number or their rank in the dissenting interest, he has most effectually defeated his own intentions, as scarce any thing could give them a meaner opinion of that party, in both these respects, than this publication of its champion.

The sermon he has obtruded upon the public is filled with paradoxes of so singular a complexion, and so feebly supported, that I find it difficult to lay hold of any thing in the form of argument, with sufficient steadiness for the purpose of discussion.

I shall endeavour, however, with as much distinctness as I am able, to select the fundamental principles on which the discourse rests, and shall attempt, as I proceed, to demonstrate their falshood and danger.

Mr. Clayton's favourite maxim is the inconsistency of the Christian profession with political science, and the certain injury its spirit and temper must sustain from every kind of interference with the affairs of government. Political subjects he considers as falling within the *peculiar* province of the irreligious; ministers in particular, he maintains, should ever observe, amidst the concussions of party, an entire neutrality, or if at any time they depart from this their natural line of conduct, it should only be in defence of the measures of government

ment in allaying diffenfions, and in convincing the people they are incompetent judges of their rights. Thefe are the fervile maxims that run through the whole of this extraordinary difcourfe; and that I may give a kind of method to the following obfervations upon them, I fhall fhew in the firft place the relation chriftianity bears to civil government, and its confiftency with political difcuffion, as conducted either by ordinary Chriftians or Minifters; in the next place, I fhall examine fome of the pretences on which the author founds his principles.

SECTION I.

On the Duty of common Chriftians in Relation to civil Policy.

THE momentous errors Mr. Clayton has committed, appear to me to have arifen from an inattention to the proper defign of chriftianity, and the place and ftation it was intended to occupy. On this fubject I beg

beg the reader's attention to the following remarks:

1st. Christianity was subsequent to the existence and creation of man. It is an institution intended to improve and ennoble our nature, not by subverting its constitution, or its powers, but by giving us a more enlarged view of the designs of Providence, and opening a prospect into eternity. As the existence of man is not to be *dated* from the publication of christianity, so neither is that order of things that flows from his relation to the present world altered or impaired by that divine system of religion. Man, under the Christian dispensation, is not a new structure erected on the ruin of the former; he may rather be compared to an ancient fabric, restored, when it had fallen into decay, and beautified afresh by the hand of its original founder. Since christianity has made its appearance in the world, he has continued the same kind of being he was before, fills the same scale in the order of existence, and is distinguished

tinguished by the same propensities and powers.

In short, christianity is not a re-organization of the principles of man, but an institution for his improvement. Hence it follows, that whatever rights are founded on the constitution of human nature, cannot be diminished or impaired by the introduction of revealed religion, which occupies itself entirely on the interests of a future world, and takes no share in the concerns of the present in any other light than as it is a state of preparation and trial. Christianity is a discovery of a future life, and acquaints us with the means by which its happiness may be secured; civil government is altogether an affair of the present state, and is no more than a provision of human skill designed to ensure freedom and tranquillity during our continuance on this temporary stage of existence. Between institutions so different in their nature and their object, it is plain no real opposition can subsist; and if ever they are represented in this light, or held inconsistent

with

with each other, it muſt proceed from an ignorance of their reſpective genius and functions. Our relation to this world demands the exiſtence of civil government; our relation to a future renders us dependant on the aid of the Chriſtian inſtitution; ſo that in reality there is no kind of contrariety between them, but each may continue without interference in its full operation. Mr. Clayton however, in ſupport of his abſurd and pernicious tenets, always takes care to place civil government and chriſtianity in oppoſition, whilſt he repreſents the former as carrying in it ſomewhat antichriſtian and prophane. Thus he informs us, *that civil government is a ſtage erected on which man acts out his character, and ſhews great depravity of heart.* All interference in political parties, he ſtiles *an alliance with the world, a neglecting to maintain our ſeparation, and to ſtand upon our own hallowed ground. There is one way,* ſays he, by which he means to inſinuate there is only one, *in which you may all interfere in the government of your country, and that is by*

prayer

prayer to God, by whom kings reign. These passages imply that the principles of civil polity and religion must be at perpetual variance, as without this supposition, unsupported as it is in fact, they can have no force or meaning.

2d. Mr. Clayton misleads his reader by not distinguishing the innocent entertainments or social duties of our nature from those acts of piety which fall within the *immediate province* of christianity.

The employments of our particular calling, the social ties and endearments of life, the improvement of the mind by liberal inquiry, and the cultivation of science and of art, form, it is true, no part of the Christian system, for they flourished before it was known; but they are intimately connected with the happiness and dignity of the human race. A Christian should act ever consistent with his profession, but he need not always be attending to the peculiar duties of it. The profession of religion does not oblige us to relinquish any undertaking on account of its being *worldly*, for we muſt then go out of the world; it is ſufficient, that every thing in which we engage, is of ſuch a nature, as will not violate the principles of virtue, or occupy ſo much of our time or attention, as may interfere with more ſacred and important duties.

Mr. Clayton obſerves, *Jeſus Chriſt uniformly waved intereſting himſelf in temporal affairs, eſpecially in the concerns of the then exiſting government*; and hence he draws a precedent to regulate the conduct of his followers. That our Saviour did not intermeddle with the policy of nations, I am as willing as our author to admit; for the improvement of this, any more than any other ſcience which might be extremely ſhort and defective, formed no part of his miſſion, and was rendered beſide quite unneceſſary, by that energy of mind which, prompted by curioſity, by our paſſions and our wants, will ever be abundantly ſufficient to perpetuate and refine every civil or human inſtitution. He never intended that his followers, on becoming Chriſtians,

ſhould

should forget they were men, or confider themselves as idle or uninterested spectators on the great theatre of life. The author's selection of proofs is almost ever unhappy, but in no instance more than the present, when he attempts to establish his doctrine of the unlawfulness of a Christian interfering in the administration of government on our Saviour's silence respecting it, a circumstance of itself sufficient to support a quite contrary conclusion; for if it had been his intention to discountenance the study of political subjects, he would have furnished us, without doubt, with some general regulations, some stated form of policy, which should for ever preclude the necessity of such discussion; or if that were impracticable, have let us into the great secret of living without government; or, lastly, have supplied its place, by a theocracy similar to that of the Jews. Nothing of this has he accomplished, and we may therefore rest assured, the political affairs of nations are suffered to remain in their ancient channels, and to be conducted as occasions may arise, by Christians or by others, without distinction.

3d, The principles of freedom ought, in a more peculiar manner, to be cherished by Christians, because they alone can secure that liberty of conscience, and freedom of inquiry, which is essential to the proper discharge of the duties of their profession. A full toleration of religious opinions, and the protection of all parties in their respective modes of worship, are the natural operations of a free government; and every thing that tends to check or restrain them, materially effects the interests of religion. Aware of the force of religious belief over the mind of man, of the generous independence it inspires, and of the eagerness with which it is cherished and maintained, it is towards this quarter the arm of despotism first directs its attacks, while through every period, the imaginary right of ruling the conscience, has been the earliest assumed, and the latest relinquished. Under this conviction, an enlightened Christian, when he turns his attention

tion to political occurrences, will rejoice in beholding every advance towards freedom in the government of nations, as it forms not only a barrier to the encroachments of tyranny, but a security to the diffusion and establishment of truth. A considerable portion of personal freedom may be enjoyed, it is true, under a despotic government, or, in other words, a great part of human actions may be left uncontrouled, but with this an enlightened mind will never rest satisfied, because it is at best but an indulgence flowing from motives of policy, or the lenity of the prince, which may be at any time withdrawn by the hand that bestowed it. Upon the same principles, religious toleration may have an accidental and precarious existence, in states whose policy is the most arbitrary; but, in such a situation, it seldom lasts long, and can never rest upon a secure and permanent basis, disappearing for the most part along with those temporary views of interest or policy, on which it was founded. The history

history of every age will attest the truth of this observation.

Mr. Clayton, in order to prepare us to digest his principles, tells us in the first page of his discourse, *that the gospel dispensation is spiritual, the worship it enjoins is simple and easy, and if liberty of conscience be granted, all its exterior order may be regarded under every kind of human government.* This is very true, but it is saying no more, than that the christian worship may be always carried on, if it is not interrupted, a point, I presume, no one will contend with him. The question is, can every form of government furnish a *security* for liberty of conscience; or, which is the same thing, can the rights of private judgment be safe under a government, whose professed principle is, that the subject has no *rights at all*, but is a vassal dependent upon his superior lord. Nor is this a futile or chimerical question, it is founded upon fact. The state to which it alludes, is the condition at present of more than half the nations of Europe; and if there were

were no better patriots than this author, it would foon be the condition of them all. The bleffings which we eftimate highly, we are naturally eager to perpetuate, and whoever is acquainted with the value of religious freedom, will not be content to fufpend it on the clemency of a prince, the indulgence of minifters, or the liberality of bifhops, if ever fuch a thing exifted; he will never think it fecure, till it has a conftitutional bafis; nor even then, till by the general fpread of its principles, every individual becomes its guarantee, and every arm ready to be lifted up in its defence. Forms of policy may change, or they may furvive the fpirit that produced them; but when the feeds of knowledge have been once fown, and have taken root in the human mind, they will advance with a fteady growth, and even flourifh in thofe alarming fcenes of anarchy and confufion, in which the fettled order and regular machinery of government, are wrecked and difappear.

Chrif-

Christianity, we see then, instead of weakening our attachment to the principles of freedom, or withdrawing them from our attention, renders them doubly dear to us, by giving us an interest in them, proportioned to the value of those religious privileges they secure and protect.

Mr. Clayton endeavours to cast reproach on the advocates for liberty, by attempting to discredit their piety, for which purpose he assures us, to be active in this cause is disreputable, and brings the reality of our religion into just suspicion. " *Who are the persons,* he asks, *that embark? Are they the spiritual, humble, and useful teachers, who travel in birth, till Christ be formed in the hearts of their hearers? No. They are philosophical opposers of the grand peculiarities of christianity.*" It is of little consequence of what descriptions of persons the friends of freedom consist, provided their principles are just, and their arguments well founded; but here, as in other places, the author displays an utter ignorance of facts. Men who know no age but their own, muſt draw their precedents from it; or if Mr. Clayton had glanced only towards the Hiſtory of England, he muſt have remembered, that in the reign of Charles the Firſt and Second, the chief friends of freedom were the Puritans, of whom many were Republicans, and the remainder zealouſly attached to a *limited* monarchy. It is to the diſtinguiſhed exertions of this party, we are in a great meaſure indebted for the preſervation of our free and happy conſtitution. In thoſe diſtracted and turbulent times, which preceded the reſtoration of Charles the Second, the Puritans, who to a devotion the moſt fervent, united an eager attachment to the doctrines of grace, as they are commonly called, diſplayed on every occaſion a love of freedom, puſhed almoſt to exceſs; whilſt the cavaliers, their opponents, who ridiculed all that was ſerious, and if they had any religion at all, held ſentiments directly repugnant to the tenets of Calvin, were the firm ſupporters of arbitrary power. If the Unitarians then are at preſent diſtinguiſhed

tinguished for their zeal in the cause of freedom, it cannot be imputed to any alliance between their religious and political opinions, but to the conduct natural to a minority, who attempting bold innovations, and maintaining sentiments very different from those which are generally held, are sensible they can only shelter themselves from persecution and reproach, and gain an impartial hearing from the public, by throwing down the barriers of prejudice, and claiming an unlimited freedom of thought.

4th, Though Christianity does not assume any immediate direction in the affairs of government, it inculcates those duties, and recommends that spirit, which will ever prompt us to cherish the principles of freedom. It teaches us to check every selfish passion, to consider ourselves as parts of a great community, and to abound in all the fruits of an active benevolence. The particular operation of this principle, will be regulated by circumstances as they arise, but our obligation to cultivate it is clear

clear and indubitable. As this author does not pretend, the nature of a government has no connexion with the felicity of those who are the subjects of it, he cannot without the utmost inconsistence deny, that to watch over the interests of our fellow-creatures in this respect, is a branch of the great duty of social benevolence. If we are bound to protect a neighbour, or even an enemy, from violence, to give him raiment when he is naked, or food when he is hungry, much more ought we to do our part, toward the preservation of a free government; the only basis on which the enjoyment of these blessings can securely rest. He who breaks the fetters of slavery, and delivers a nation from thraldom, forms, in my opinion, the noblest comment on the great law of love, whilst he distributes the greatest blessing which man can receive from man; but next to that is the merit of him, who in times like the present, watches over the edifice of public liberty, repairs its foundations, and strengthens its

cement,

cement, when he beholds it haftening to decay.

It is not in the power of every one, it is true, to benefit his age, or country, in this diftinguifhed manner, and accordingly it is no where exprefsly commanded; but where this ability exifts, it is not diminifhed by our embracing chriftianity, which confecrates every talent to the public good. On whomfoever diftinguifhed endowments are beftowed, as Chriftians we ought to rejoice, when inftead of being wafted in vain or frivolous purfuits, we behold them employed on objects of the greateft general concern; amongft which thofe principles of freedom will ever be reckoned, which determine the deftiny of nations, and the collective felicity of the human race.

5th, Mr. Clayton expreffes an ardent defire for the approach of that period, when all men will be Chriftians. I have no doubt that this event will take place, and rejoice in the profpect of it; but whenever it arrives, it will be fatal to Mr. Clayton's favorite principles; for the profeffors of chriftianity muſt then become politicians, as the wicked, on whom he at preſent very politely devolves the buſineſs of government, will be no more: or, perhaps, he indulges a hope, that even then, there will be a ſufficient number of ſinners left, to conduct political affairs, eſpecially as wars will then ceaſe, and ſocial life be leſs frequently diſturbed by rapine and injuſtice. It will ſtill, however, be a great hardſhip, that a handful of the wicked ſhould rule innumerable multitudes of the juſt, and cannot fail, according to our preſent conceptions, to operate as a kind of check on piety and virtue. How Mr. Clayton will ſettle this point I cannot pretend to ſay, except he imagines, men will be able to ſubſiſt without any laws or civil regulations, or intends to revive the long exploded tradition of Papias, reſpecting the perſonal reign.

Had chriſtianity been intended only for the benefit of a few, or as the diſtinction of a ſmall fraternity, there might have been ſome pretence, for ſetting its profeſſion in

oppo-

opposition to human policy, since it might then have been conducted without their interference; but a religion, which is formed for the whole world, and will finally be embraced by all its inhabitants, can never be clogged with any such impediment, as would render it repugnant to the social existence of mankind.

SECTION II.

On the Duty of Ministers in Respect to civil Polity.

MR. CLAYTON is extremely severe upon those of his brethren, who, forsaking the quiet duties of their profession, as he stiles them, have dared to interfere in public affairs. This he considers as a most flagrant offence, an alarming departure from their proper province, and in the fullness of his rage, he heaps upon them every epithet, which contempt, or indignation can suggest; calls them meddling, convivial, political ministers, devoid of all seriousness

riousness and dignity. It is rather extraordinary, this severe correction should be administered by a man, who is, at that moment, guilty of the offence he is chastizing; reproaches political preachers in a political sermon; ridicules theories of government, and at the same time advances one of his own, a most wretched one indeed, but delivered in a tone the most arrogant and decisive. It is not political discussion then, it seems, that has ruffled the gentle serenity of our author's temper; for he too, we see, can bend, when it pleases him, from his spiritual elevation, and let fall his oracular responses on the duty of subjects and of kings. But the persons on whom he denounces his anathemas, have presumed to adopt a system of politics inconsistent with his own, and it is less his piety than his pride, that is shocked and offended. Instead of submitting to be moulded by any adept in cringes, any posture-master of servility, they have dared to assume the bold and natural port of freemen.

It will be unnecessary to say much on the duty of ministers, in respect to political affairs, as many of the reflections which this subject would suggest, have been already advanced under a former head. A few considerations, however, present themselves here, to which I shall beg the reader's attention.

The duties of the ministerial character, it will on all hands be confessed, are of a nature the most sacred and important. To them should be directed the first and chief attention of every person who sustains it, and whatever is found to interfere with these momentous engagements, should be relinquished as criminal and improper. But there is no profession which occupies the mind so fully, as not to leave many intervals of leisure, in which objects that lie out of its immediate province, will have a share of our attention; and I see not, why these periods of recess may not be employed with as much dignity and advantage, in acquiring an acquaintance with the principles of government, as wasted in frivolous

volous amufements, or an inactive indolence. Mr. Clayton, with his ufual confidence, lays it down as a maxim, that the fcience of politics cannot be cultivated, without a neglect of minifterial duties; and one would almoft be tempted to fuppofe, he had publifhed his fermon as a confirmation of this remark, as a more ftriking example of political ignorance in a teacher of religion, has fcarce ever been exhibited. As far, therefore, as the preacher himfelf is concerned, the obfervation will be admitted in its full force, but he has furely no right to make his own weaknefs the ftandard of another's ftrength.

Political fcience, as far as it falls under our prefent contemplation, may be confidered in two points of view. It may either intend a difcuffion of the great objects for which governments are formed, or it may intend a confideration of the means which may be employed, and the particular contrivances that may be fallen upon to accomplifh thofe objects. For example, in vindicating the revolution in France, two dif-

E   tinct

tinct methods may be purfued with equal propriety and fuccefs. It may be defended upon its *principles* againft the friends of arbitrary power, by difplaying the value of freedom, the equal rights of mankind, the folly and injuftice of thofe regal or ariftocratic pretenfions, by which thofe rights were invaded; accordingly, in this light it has been juftified with the utmoft fuccefs. Or it may be defended upon its *expedients*, by exhibiting the elements of government which it has compofed, the laws it has enacted, and the tendency of both, to extend and perpetuate that liberty which is its ultimate object. But though each of thefe modes of difcuffion fall within the province of politics, it is obvious, the degree of enquiry, of knowledge, and of labour they require, differs widely. The firft is a path which has been often and fuccefsfully trod, turns upon principles which are common to all times and places, and which demand little elfe to enforce conviction, than calm and difpaffionate attention. The latter method involving a queftion of expediency,

pediency, not of right, would lead into a vaſt field of detail, would require a thorough acquaintance with the ſituation of perſons and of things, as well as long and intimate acquaintance with human affairs. There are but few miniſters who have capacity or leiſure to become great practical politicians. To explore the intricacies of commercial ſcience, to penetrate the refinements of negociation, to determine with certainty and preciſion the balance of power, are undertakings, it will be confeſſed, which lie very remote from the miniſterial department; but the *principles* of government, as it is a contrivance for ſecuring the freedom and happineſs of men, may be acquired with great eaſe.

Theſe principles our anceſtors underſtood well, and it would be no ſmall ſhame, if, in an age which boaſts ſo much light and improvement, they were leſs familiar to us. There is no claſs of men to whom this ſpecies of knowledge is ſo requiſite, on ſeveral accounts, as diſſenting miniſters. The jealous policy of the eſtabliſhment,

forbids our youth admiffion into the celebrated feats of learning; our own feminaries, at leaft, till lately, were almoft entirely confined to candidates for the miniftry; and as on both thefe accounts, amongft us, the intellectual improvement of our religious teachers, rifes fuperior to that of private chriftians, in a greater degree than in the national church; the influence of their opinions is wider in proportion. Difclaiming as they do, all pretenfions to dominion, their public character, their profeffional leifure, the habits of ftudy and compofition which they acquire, concur to point them out as the natural guardians, in fome meafure, of our liberties and rights. Befides, as they are appointed to teach the whole compafs of focial duty, the mutual obligations of rulers and fubjects, will, of neceffity, fall under their notice, and they cannot explain or enforce the *reafons* of fubmiffion, without difplaying the *proper end* of government, and the *expectations* we may naturally form from it; which, when accurately done, will
lead

lead into the very depths of political science.

There is another reason, however, diſtinct from any I have yet mentioned, flowing from the nature of an eſtabliſhed religion, why diſſenting miniſters, above all men, ſhould be well ſkilled in the principles of freedom. Wherever, as in England, religion is eſtabliſhed by law with ſplendid emoluments and dignities, annexed to its profeſſion, the Clergy, who are candidates for theſe diſtinctions, will ever be prone to exalt the prerogative, not only in order to ſtrengthen the arm on which they lean, but that they may the more ſucceſsfully ingratiate themſelves in the favour of the Prince, by flattering thoſe ambitious views and paſſions which are too readily entertained by perſons poſſeſſed of ſupreme power. The boaſted alliance between church and ſtate, on which ſo many encomiums have been laviſhed, ſeems to have been little more than a compact between the Prieſt and the Magiſtrate, to betray the liberties of mankind, both civil and religious.

ous. To this the Clergy on their part at leaft have continued fteady, fhunning enquiry, fearful of change, blind to the corruptions of government, fkilful to *difcern the figns of the times*, and eager to improve every opportunity, and to employ all their art and eloquence to extend the prerogative, and fmooth the approaches of arbitrary power. Individuals are illuftrious exceptions to this cenfure; it however applies to the body, to none more than to thofe whofe exalted rank and extenfive influence determine its complexion and fpirit. In this fituation, the leaders of that church, in their fatal attempt to recommend and embellifh a flavifh fyftem of principles, will, I truft, be ever carefully watched and oppofed by thofe who hold a fimilar ftation amongft the diffenters; that, at all events, there may remain one afylum to which infulted freedom may retire unmolefted. Thefe confiderations are fufficient to juftify every diffenting minifter in well-timed exertions for the public caufe, and from them we may learn what opinion to entertain

tertain of Mr. Clayton's weak and malignant invectives.

From the general strain of his discourse it would be natural to conclude he was an enemy to every interference of ministers on political occasions; but this is not the case. *Ministers*, says he, *may interfere as peacemakers, and by proper methods should counteract the spirit of faction raised by persons who seem born to vex the state.* After having taught them to remain in a quiet neutrality, he invests them all at once with the high character of arbiters between the contending parties, without considering that an office of so much delicacy would demand a most intimate acquaintance with the pretensions of both. Ministers it should seem, instead of declining political interference, are to become such adepts in the science of government, as to distinguish with precision the complaints of an oppressed party, from the clamours of a faction, to hold the balance between the ruler and the subject with a steady hand, *and to point out, on every occasion, and counteract the persons who*

are

are born to vex the state. If any should demand by what means they are to furnish themselves for such extraordinary undertakings, he will learn it is not by political investigation or enquiry this profound skill is to be attained, but by a studied inattention and neglect, of which this author, it must be confessed, has given his Disciples a most edifying example in his first essay. There is something miraculous in these endowments. This battle is not to the strong, nor these riches to men of understanding. Our author goes a step farther, for when he is in the humour for concessions no man can be more liberal. *So far as revolutions,* says he, *are parts of God's plan of government, a Christian is not to hinder such changes in states as promise an increase of happiness to mankind. But no where in the New Testament can a Christian find countenance in becoming a forward active man in regenerating the civil constitutions of nations.* A Christian is not to oppose revolutions, as far as they are parts of God's plan of government. The direction which

oracles

oracles afford, has ever been complained of for its obfcurity; and this of Mr. Clayton, though no doubt it is fraught with the profoundeft wifdom, would have been more ufeful had it furnifhed fome criterion to diftinguifh thofe tranfactions which *are* parts of God's plan of government. We have hitherto imagined the elements of nature, and the whole agency of man, are comprehended within the fyftem of divine Providence; but as in this fenfe every thing becomes a part of the divine plan, it cannot be his meaning. Perhaps he means to confine the phrafe *of God's plan of government* to that portion of human agency which is confiftent with the divine will and promifes, as he fays an increafe of happinefs to mankind. If this fhould be his intention, the fentiment is juft, but utterly fubverfive of the purpofe for which it is introduced, as it concurs with the principle of all reformers in leaving us no other direction in thefe cafes, than reafon and experience, determined in their exertions, by a regard to the general happinefs of mankind.

mankind. On this basis the wildest projectors profess to erect their improvements. On this principle too do the dissenters proceed, when they call for a repeal of the test act, when they lament the unequal representation of parliament, when they wish to see a period to ministerial corruption, and to the encroachments of an hierarchy equally servile and oppressive; and thus by one unlucky concession this author has admitted the ground-work of reform in its fullest extent, and has demolished the whole fabrick he was so eager to rear. He must not be offended if principles thus corrupt, and thus feebly supported, should meet with the contempt they deserve, but must seek his consolation in his own adage, as the correction of folly is certainly *a part of God's plan of government*. The reader can be at no loss to determine, whom the author intends by a *busy active man in regenerating the civil constitutions of nations*. The occasion of the sermon, and complexion of its sentiments, concur in directing us to Dr. Priestley; a person

person whom the author seems to regard with a more than *odium theologicum*, with a rancour exceeding the measure even of his profession. The religious tenets of Dr. Priestley, appear to me erroneous in the extreme, but I should be sorry to suffer any difference of sentiment to diminish my sensibility to virtue, or my admiration of genius. From him the poisoned arrow will fall pointless. His enlightened and active mind, his unwearied assiduity, the extent of his researches, the light he has poured into almost every department of science, will be the admiration of that period, when the greater part of those who have favoured, or those who have opposed him, will be alike forgotten. Distinguished merit will ever rise superior to oppression, and will draw lustre from reproach. The vapours which gather round the rising sun, and follow it in its course, seldom fail at the close of it to form a magnificent theatre for its reception, and to invest with variegated tints, and with a softened effulgence the luminary which they cannot hide.

It is a pity, however, our author in reproaching characters so illustrious was not a little more attentive to facts; for unfortunately for him Dr. Priestley has not in any instance displayed that disaffection to government, with which he has been charged so wantonly. In his Lectures on History, and his Essay on civil Government, which of all his publications fall most properly within the sphere of politicks, he has delineated the British constitution with great accuracy, and has expressed his warm admiration of it as the best system of policy the sagacity of man has been able to contrive. In his Familiar Letters to the Inhabitants of Birmingham, a much later work, where the seeds of that implacable dislike were scattered which produced the late riots, he has renewed that declaration, and has informed us, that he has been pleasantly ridiculed by his friends as being an Unitarian in religion, and a Trinitarian in politicks. He has lamented, indeed, in common with every enlightened citizen, the existence of certain corruptions, which being

ing gradually introduced into the conſtitution, have greatly impaired its vigour; but in this he has had the honour of being followed by the prime miniſter himſelf, who began his career by propoſing a reform in parliament, merely to court popularity it is true, at a time when it would not have been ſo ſafe for him to inſult the friends of freedom after having betrayed their intereſt, as he has ſince found it.

Dr. Prieſtley has, moreover, defended with great ability and ſucceſs the principles of our diſſent, expoſing, as the very nature of the undertaking demands, the folly and injuſtice of all clerical uſurpations; and on this account, if on no other, he is entitled to the gratitude of his brethren. In addition to this catalogue of crimes, he has ventured to expreſs his ſatisfaction on the liberation of France; an event, which, promiſing a firmer eſtabliſhment to liberty than any recorded in the annals of the world, is contemplated by the friends of arbitrary power throughout every kingdom of Europe with the utmoſt concern. Theſe are the
demerits

demerits of Dr. Prieftley, for which this political aftrologift and facred calculator of nativities, pronounces upon him that he is *born to vex the ftate.* The beft apology candour can fuggeft, will be to hope Mr. Clayton has never read Dr. Prieftley's political works; a conjecture fomewhat confirmed from his difclaiming all attention to political theories, and from the extreme ignorance he difplays through the whole of his difcourfe on political topics. Still it is to be wifhed he would have condefcended to underftand what he meant to confute, if it had been only to fave himfelf the trouble and difgrace of this publication.

The manner in which he fpeaks of the Birmingham riots, and the caufe to which he traces them, are too remarkable to pafs unnoticed.

When led, fays he, fpeaking of the fufferers, *by officious zeal, from the quiet duties of their profeffion, into the Senator's province: unhallowed boifterous paffions in others; like their own, God may permit to chaftife them.* For my own part I was fome time before
I could

I could develope this extraordinary paſſage; but I now find the darkneſs in which it is veiled is no more than that myſtic ſublimity, which has always tinctured the language of thoſe who are appointed to interpret the counſels of heaven.

I would not have Mr. Clayton deal too freely in theſe viſions, leſt the fire and illumination of the prophet ſhould put out the reaſon of the man, a caution the more neceſſary in the preſent inſtance, as it glimmers ſo feebly already in ſeveral parts of his diſcourſe, that its extinction would not be at all extraordinary. We are, no doubt, much obliged to Mr. Clayton for letting us into a ſecret we could never have learnt any other way. We thank him heartily for informing us, the Birmingham riots were a judgment, and, as we would wiſh to be grateful for ſuch an important communication, we would whiſper in his ear in return, that he ſhould be particularly careful not to ſuffer this itch of propheſying to grow upon him, men being extremely apt in this degenerate age to miſtake a prophet for

for a madman, and to lodge them in the same place of confinement. The best use he could make of his mantle would be to bequeath it to the use of posterity, as for the want of it I am afraid they will be in danger of falling into some very unhappy mistakes. To their unenlightened eyes it will appear a reproach, that in the eighteenth century, an age that boasts its science and improvement, the first philosopher in Europe, of a character unblemished, and of manners the most mild and gentle, should be torn from his family, and obliged to flee an outcast and a fugitive from the murderous hands of a frantic rabble; but when they learn that there were not wanting teachers of religion, who secretly triumphed in these barbarities, they will pause for a moment, and imagine they are reading the history of Goths or of Vandals. Erroneous as such a judgment must appear in the eyes of Mr. Clayton, nothing but a ray of his supernatural light could enable us to form a juster decision. Dr. Priestley and his friends are not the

first

first that have suffered in a public cause; and when we recollect, that those who have sustained similar disasters have been generally conspicuous for a superior sanctity of character, what but an acquaintance with the counsels of Heaven can enable us to distinguish between these two classes of sufferers, and whilst one are the favourites of God, to discern in the other the objects of his vengeance. When we contemplate this extraordinary endowment, we are no longer surprized at the superiority he assumes through the whole of his discourse, nor at that air of confusion and disorder which appears in it, both of which we impute to his dwelling so much in the insufferable light, and amidst the coruscations and flashes of the divine glory; a sublime but perilous situation, described with great force and beauty by Mr. Gray.

> " He passed the flaming bounds of place and time:
> " The living throne, the sapphire blaze,
> " Where Angels tremble, while they gaze,
> " He saw; but blasted with excess of light,
> " Closed his eyes in endless night."

SECTION III.

On the Pretences Mr. Clayton advances in favour of his Principles.

HAVING endeavoured to juftify the well timed exertions of Chriftians and of Minifters, in the caufe of freedom, it may not be improper to examine a little more particularly under what pretences Mr. Clayton prefumes to condemn this conduct.

1ft. The firft that naturally prefents itfelf, is drawn from thofe paffages of fcripture, in which the defign of civil government is explained, and the duty of fubmiffion to civil authority is enforced. That on which the greateft ftrefs is laid, is found in the ninth chapter of the Epiftle to the Romans. " Let every foul be fubject to
" the higher powers; for there is no power
" but of God: the powers which are, are
" ordained of God. Whoever therefore
" refifteth the power, refifteth the ordi-
" nance of God; and they that refift, fhall
" receive

" receive unto themfelves damnation. The
" Ruler is the Minifter of God to thee for
" good. But if thou doeft that which is
" evil, be afraid, for he beareth not the
" fword in vain. Wherefore ye muft be
" fubject not only for wrath, but con-
" fcience fake." This paffage, which, from
the time of Sir Robert Filmer to the prefent day, has been the ftrong hold of the
doctrine of paffive obedience and non-re-
fiftance, will admit of an eafy folution, by
attending to the nature of chriftianity, and
the circumftances of its profeffors, during
the period it was written. The extraordinary privileges and dignity conferred by
the Gofpel on believers, muft have affected
the minds of the firft Chriftians, juft
emerging from the fhades of ignorance,
and awakened to new hopes, with fingular
force. Feeling an elevation to which they
were ftrangers before, and looking down
upon the world around them, as the vaffals
of fin and fatan, they might be eafily
tempted to imagine, the reftraint of laws
could not extend to perfons fo highly privileged,

vileged, and that it was ignominious in the free men of Jesus Christ, to submit to the yoke of idolatrous rulers. Natural to their situation as these sentiments might be, none could be conceived of more detrimental to the credit and propagation of a rising religion, or more likely to draw down upon its professors the whole weight of the Roman empire, with which they were in no condition to contend. In this situation, it was proper for the Apostle, to remind Christians, their religion did not interfere with the rights of princes, or diminish their obligation to attend to those salutary regulations, which are established for the protection of innocence, and the punishment of the guilty. That this only was the intention of the writer, may be inferred from the considerations he adduces to strengthen his advice. He does not draw his arguments for submission from any thing *peculiar* to the *christian system*, as he must have done, had he intended to oppose that religion to the natural rights of mankind, but from the utility and necessity

of

of civil reftraints. The Ruler is the Minifter of God to thee for good, is the reafon he urges for fubmiffion. Civil government, as if he had faid, is a falutary inftitution, appointed to reftrain and punifh outrage and injuftice, but exhibiting to the quiet and inoffenfive, nothing of which they need to be afraid. If thou doeft that which is evil, be afraid, for he beareth not the "*fword in vain.*" He is an avenger to execute wrath upon him that doeth evil. Chriftians were not to confider themfelves privileged above their fellow-citizens, as their religion conferred upon them no civil immunities, but left them fubject to all the ties and reftraints, whatever they were, which could be juftly impofed by the civil power, or any other part of mankind.

The limits of every duty muft be determined by its *reafons*, and the only ones affigned *here*, or that *can* be affigned for fubmiffion to civil authority, are its *tendency to do good*; wherever therefore this fhall ceafe to be the cafe, fubmiffion becomes abfurd, absurd, having no longer any *rational view*. But at what time this evil shall be judged to have arrived, or what remedy it may be proper to apply, christianity does not decide, but leaves to be determined, by an appeal to natural reason and right. By one of the strongest misconceptions in the world, when we are taught that christianity does not bestow upon us any *new* rights, it has been thought to strip us of our *old*; which is just the same as it would be to conclude, because it did not first furnish us with hands or feet, it obliges us to cut them off.

Under every form of government, that civil order which affords protection to property, and tranquillity to individuals, must be obeyed; and I have no doubt, that before the revolution in France, they who are now its warmest admirers, had they lived there, would have yielded a quiet submission to its laws, as being conscious, the social compact can only be considered as dissolved, by an expression of the general will. In the mean time, they would have continued firm in avowing the principles

ciples of freedom, and by the spread of political knowledge, have endeavoured to train and prepare the minds of their fellow-citizens, for accomplishing a change so desirable.

It is not necessary to enter into a particular examination of the other texts, adduced by Mr. Clayton in support of his sentiments, as this in Romans is by much the most to his purpose, and the remarks that have been made upon it may, with very little alteration, be applied to the rest. He refers us to the second chapter of the first epistle of Peter. " Submit yourselves
" to every ordinance of man for the Lord's
" sake; whether it be to the King as su-
" preme, or unto Governors as unto them,
" that are sent by him, for the punish-
" ment of evil doers, and for the praise of
" them that do well." Here it is sufficient to remark, all that can be inferred from this passage is, that Christians are not to hold themselves exempt from the obligation of obedience on account of their religion,

but

but are to respect legislation as far as it is found productive of benefit in social life.

With still less propriety, he urges the first of Timothy, " where in the second " chapter, we are exhorted to supplicati- " ons, prayers, intercessions, and giving " of thanks for all men, for kings, and " for all that are in authority, that we may " lead a quiet and peaceable life, in all " godliness and honesty." I am unacquainted with any who refuse a compliance with this apostolical admonition, except the Nonjurors may be reckoned of this class, whose political sentiments are of a piece with Mr. Clayton's.

Whilst he pleads with so much eagerness for the duty of passive obedience, we are not, however, to suppose, he wishes to extend it to all mankind. He admits, *" that society, under the wisest regulations,* *" will degenerate, and there will be periods* *" when associated bodies must be resolved again* *" into its first principles."* All resistance to authority, every revolution, is not in his own opinion criminal; it is Christians only,

who

who are never to have a share in these transactions, never to assert their rights. With what different sentiments did the great apostle of the Gentiles contemplate his character, when disdaining to accept a clandestine dismission from an unjust imprisonment, he felt a glow of indignant pride burn upon his cheek, and exclaimed with a Roman energy, " I was free born!"

2d. Another reason which this author assigns for a blind deference to civil authority is, that christianity is " *distinct from,* " *and independant of human legislation.*" This principle no Protestant Dissenter will be enclined to question, but instead of lending any support to the system of passive obedience, it will overturn it from its foundation; for if religion be really distinct from, and independant of human legislation, it cannot afford any standard to ascertain its limits; as the moment it is applied to this purpose, it ceases to be a thing distinct and independent. For example, it is not doubted that a Christian may lawfully engage in trade or commerce; but if it be asked why his profession does not interfere with such an undertaking, the proper reply will be, religion is a thing distinct and independant. Should it be again inquired, why a Christian may become a trader, yet must not commit a theft, we should answer, that this latter action is not a thing distinct, or independant of religion, but falls immediately under its cognizance, as a violation of its laws. Thus it appears, that whatever portion of human conduct is really *independant* of religion, is lawful for that *very reason*, and can then only become criminal or improper, when it is suffered to intrench upon more sacred or important duties. The truth is, between two institutions, such as civil government and religion, which have a separate origin and end, no opposition can subsist, but in the brain of a distempered enthusiast.

The author's text confutes his doctrine, for had our Saviour annihilated our rights, he would have become a *judge* and *divider* over us, in the worst sense, if that could be said to be divided, which is taken away.

When

When any two inſtitutions are affirmed to be diſtinct and independant, it can only mean, they do not *interfere*; but that muſt be a genius of no common ſize, who can infer from religion not *interfering* with the rights of mankind, that they ceaſe to be, or that the patrimony, over which our Lord declined to exerciſe *any authority*, he has ſcattered and deſtroyed.

3d. Similar to the laſt I have conſidered, is that pretence for excluding Chriſtians from any concern in political affairs, taken from the conduct of our Saviour, Mr. Clayton tells us, that Chriſt uniformly waved intereſting himſelf in the concerns of the then exiſting government, and to the ſame purpoſe he afterwards remarks, he always declined the functions of a civil magiſtrate.

The moſt careleſs reader will remark, the whole weight of this argument reſts upon a ſuppoſition, that it is unlawful for a Chriſtian to ſuſtain any other character in civil life, than that in which our Saviour literally appeared; a notion as extravagant as was ever nourished in the brain of the wildest fanatic. Upon this principle he must have gone through such a succession of offices, and engaged in such an endless variety of undertakings, that in place of thirty-three years, he needed to have lived thirty-three centuries. On this ground the profession of physic is unlawful for a Christian, because our Lord never set up a dispensary; and that of law, because he never pleaded at the bar. Next to the weakness of advancing such absurdity, is that of confuting it.

4th. The author, in proof of his political tenets, appeals to the devotional feelings of his hearers. " I ask you, says he, " who make conscience of entering into " your closets, and shutting your doors, " and praying to your Father which seeth " in secret; what subjects interest you most " then? Are not factious passions hushed; " the undue heat you felt in political dis- " putation, remembered with sorrow!" He must be at a great loss for argument, who will have recourse to such loose and

flimsy

flimsy declamation. When engaged in devout admiration of the supreme Being, every other object will be lost in the comparison; but this, though the noblest employment of the mind, was never intended to shut out all other concerns. The affections which unite us to the world, have a large demand upon us, and must succeed in their turn. If every thing is to be deemed criminal, that does not interest the attention in the very moment of worship, political concerns are not the only ones to be abandoned, but every undertaking of a temporal nature, labour and ingenuity, must cease. Science herself must shroud her light. These are notions rather to be laughed at than confuted, for their extravagance will correct itself. Every attempt that has been made to rear religion on the ruins of nature, or to render it subversive of the œconomy of life, has hitherto proved unsuccessful, whilst the institutions that have flowed from it, are now scarcely regarded in any other light, than as humiliating monuments of human weakness and folly.

folly. The natural vigour of the mind, when it has once been opened by knowledge, and turned towards great and interesting objects, will always overpower the illusions of fanaticism; or could Mr. Clayton's principles be carried into effect, we should soon behold men returning again to the state of a savage, and a more than monkish barbarity and ignorance would overspread the earth. That abstraction from the world, it is his purpose to recommend, is in truth as inconsistent with the nature of religion, as with the state and condition of man, for christianity does not propose to take us *out* of the world, but to preserve us from the pollutions which are *in* it.

It is easy to brand a passion for liberty with the odious epithet of faction; no two things, however, can be more opposite. Faction is a combination of a few to oppress the liberties of many; the love of freedom is the impulse of an enlightened and presiding spirit, ever intent upon the welfare of the community, or body to which it belongs, and ready to give the alarm,

alarm, when it beholds any unlawful conspiracy formed, whether it be of rulers or of subjects, with a design to oppress it. Every tory upholds a faction; every whig, as far as he is sincere and well informed, is a friend to the equal liberties of mankind. Absurd as the preacher's appeal must appear, on such an occasion, to the devout feelings of his hearers, we have no need to decline it. In these solemn moments, factious passions cannot indeed be too much hushed, but that warmth which animates the patriot, which glowed in the breast of a Sidney or a Hampden, was never chilled, or diminished, we may venture to affirm, in its nearest approaches to the uncreated splendour; and if it mingled with their devotion at all, could not fail to infuse into it a fresh force and vigour, by drawing them into a closer assimilation to that great Being, who appears under the character of the avenger of the oppressed, and the friend and protector of the human race.

5th, Lastly, the author endeavours to discredit the principles of freedom, by holding

ing them up as intimately connected with the Unitarian herefy. " We are not to be " furprized, he fays, if men who vacate " the rule of faith in Jefus Chrift, fhould " be defective in deference, and in obedi- " ent regards to men, who are raifed to " offices of fuperior influence, for the pur- " pofes of civil order and public good." The perfons he has in view are the Unitarians, and that my reader may be in full pofleffion of this moft curious argument, it may be proper to inform him, that an Unitarian is a perfon who believes Jefus Chrift had no exiftence till he appeared on our earth, whilft a Trinitarian maintains, that he exifted with the Father from all eternity. What poffible connection can he difcern between thefe opinions and the fubject of government?

In order to determine, whether the fupreme power fhould be vefted in king, lords, and commons, as in England, in an affembly of nobles as in Venice, or in a houfe of reprefentatives, as in America or France, muft we firft decide upon the perfon son of Christ. I should imagine we might as well apply to astronomy first, to learn whether the earth flattens at the poles. He explains what he means by *vacating* the rule of faith in Christ, when he charges the Unitarians with a partial denial at least, of the inspiration of the scriptures, particularly the Epistles of St. Paul. But however clear the inspiration of the scriptures may be, as no one pleads for the inspiration of civil governors, the deference which is due to the first, as coming from God, can be no reason for an unlimited submission to the latter. Yet this is Mr. Clayton's argument, and it runs thus. Every opposition to scripture is criminal, because it is inspired, and therefore every resistance to temporal rulers is criminal, though they are *not* inspired.

The number of passages in Paul's Epistles, which treat of civil government, is small, the principal of them have been examined, and whether they are inspired or not, has not the remotest relation to the question before us. The inspiration of an author

author adds weight to his sentiments, but makes no alteration in his meaning, and unless Mr. Clayton can show that Paul inculcates unlimited submission, the belief of his inspiration can yield no advantage to his cause. Amongst those parties of Christians who have maintained the inspiration of the scriptures in its utmost extent, the number of such as have inferred from them the doctrine of passive obedience, has been extremely small; it is therefore ridiculous to impute the rejection of this tenet by Unitarians, to a disbelief of plenary inspiration. It behoves Mr. Clayton to point out, if he is able, any one of the Unitarians, who ever imagined that Paul means to recommend unlimited obedience; for till that is the case, it is plain, their political opinions cannot have arisen from any contempt of that Apostle's authority.

As there is no foundation in the nature of things, for imagining any alliance between heretical tenets and the principles of freedom, this notion is equally void of support from fact or history. Were the Socinian

nian sentiments, in particular, productive of any *peculiar impatience under* the restraints of government, this effect could not fail of having made its appearance on their first rise in Poland, while their influence was fresh and vigorous, but nothing of this nature occurred, or was any such reproach cast upon them. That sect in England which has been always most conspicuous for the love of freedom, have for the most part held sentiments, at the greatest remove from Socinianism that can be imagined. The seeds of those political principles which broke out with such vigour in the reign of Charles Ist, and have since given rise to the denomination of whigs, were sown in the latter-end of the reign of Queen Elizabeth, by the hand of the puritans, amongst whom the Unitarian doctrine was then utterly unknown. The Dissenters descended from those illustrious ancestors, and inheriting their spirit, have been foremost in defence of liberty, not only, or chiefly, of late, since the spread of the Socinian doctrine,

doctrine, but before that system had gained any footing amongst us.

The knowledge and study of the scriptures, far from favouring the pretensions of despotism, have almost ever diminished it, and been attended with a proportional increase of freedom. The union of protestant Princes preserved the liberties of the Germanick body when they were in danger of being overwhelmed by the victorious arm of Charles Vth; yet a veneration for the scriptures, at a time when they had almost fallen into oblivion, and an appeal to their decisions in all points, was the grand characteristic of the new religion. If we look into Turkey, we shall find the least of that impatience under restraints, Mr. Clayton laments, of any place in the world, though Paul and his epistles are not much studied there.

There are not wanting reasons, which at first view might induce us to conclude, unitarianism was less favourable to the love of freedom than almost any other system of religious belief. If any party of Christians

were

were ever free from the leaſt tincture of enthuſiaſm, it is the unitarian: yet that paſſion has by every philoſopher been judged friendly to liberty; and to its influence, though perhaps improperly, ſome of its moſt diſtinguiſhed exertions have been aſcribed. Hume and Bolingbroke, who were Atheiſts, leaned towards arbitrary power. Owen, Howe, Milton, Baxter, ſome of the moſt devout and venerable characters that ever appeared, were warmly attached to liberty, and held ſentiments on the ſubject of government as free and unfettered as Dr. Prieſtley. Thus every pretence for confounding the attachment to freedom with the ſentiments of a religious party, is moſt abundantly confuted both from reaſon and from fact. The zeal Unitarians have diſplayed in defence of civil and religious liberty, is the ſpirit natural to a minority, who are well aware they are viewed by the eccleſiaſtical powers with an unparalleled malignity and rancour. Let the Diſſenters at large remember they too are a minority, a great minority, and that they muſt look

for

for their security from the same quarter, not from the compliments of bishops, or presents from maids of honour *.

To abandon principles, which the best and most enlightened men have in all ages held sacred, which the Dissenters in particular have rendered themselves illustrious by defending, which have been sealed and consecrated by the blood of our ancestors, for no other reason than that the Unitarians chance to maintain them, would be a weakness of which a child might be ashamed! Whoever may think fit to take up the gauntlet in the Socinian controversy will have my warmest good wishes; but let us not employ those arms against each other which were given us for our common defence.

* Some of my readers perhaps need to be informed that I here allude to Mr. Martin, who, for similar services to those Mr. Clayton is now performing, has been considerably caressed by certain bishops who have condescended to notice and to visit him. I think we do not read that Judas had any acquaintance with the high priests till he came to transact business with them.

SECTION

SECTION IV.

On the Test Act.

AMIDST all the wild excentricities, which, abounding in every part of this extraordinary publication, naturally diminish our wonder at any thing such a writer may advance, I confess I am surprised at his declaring his wish for the continuance of the Test Act. This law, enacted in the latter end of the reign of Charles IId, to secure the nation from popery, when it stood upon the brink of that precipice, is continued, now that the danger no longer exists which first occasioned it, for the express purpose of preserving the church from the inroads of Dissenters. That church, it must be remembered, existed for ages before it received any such protection; yet is it now the vogue to magnify its importance to that degree, that one would imagine it was its sole prop, whose removal would draw the whole fabrick after it, or at least

make

make it totter to its base. Whether these apprehensions were really entertained by the clergy who gave the signal for the commencement of hostilities on a late occasion, or whether they were only impelled by that illiberal tincture, and fixed antipathy to all who differ from them, which hath ever marked their character, may be doubted; but to behold a Dissenting Minister joining with them in an unnatural warfare against his brethren, is a phenomenon so curious, that it prompts us to enquire into its cause. Let us hear his reasons. He and many others were convinced, he tells us, " that
" some of the persons who applied for the
" repeal were influenced by enmity against
" the doctrinal articles of the established
" church, and they could not sacrifice their
" pious regard to truth, though in a
" church they had separated from, to the
" policy of men, who with respect to God
" our Saviour only consult how they may
" cast him down from his excellency."
When we hear the clergy exclaim that their church is in danger, we pretty well un-

derstand what they mean; they speak broad, as Mr. Burke says, and intend no more than that its emoluments are endangered; but when a serious Dissenter expresses his pious regard to the doctrines of the church, it is the *truth* of those articles he must be supposed to have in view. Let us consider for a moment what advantage the Test Act is capable of yielding them. All those who qualify for civil offices, by a submission to this law, consist of two classes of people; they are either persons who are attached to the articles of the church, from whom therefore no danger could accrue; or they are persons who have signified their assent to doctrines which they inwardly disapprove, and who have qualified themselves for trust by a solemn act of religious deception. It is this latter class alone, it should be remembered, whom the Test Act can at all influence, and thus the only security this celebrated law can afford the articles of the church, is founded in a flagrant violation of truth in the persons who become their guarantees. Every attempt that has been made to uphold religion by the civil arm, has reflected difgrace upon its authors; but of all that are recorded in the hiftory of the World, perhaps this is the moft abfurd in its principle, and the leaft effectual in its operation. For the truth of facred myfteries in religion, it appeals to the corrupteft principles of the human heart, and to thofe *only*; for no one can be tempted by the Teft Act, to profefs an attachment to the doctrines of the church, till he has been already allured by the dignity or emolument of a civil office. By compelling all who exercife any function in the ftate, from the perfon who afpires to its higheft diftinctions, to thofe who fill the meaneft offices in it, to profefs that concurrence in religious opinions which is known never to exift, it is adapted beyond any other human invention, to fpread amongft all orders of men a contempt for facred inftitutions, to inthrone hypocrify, and reduce deception to a fyftem! The truth of any fet of opinions can only be perceived by *evidence*; but what evidence can any one derive from the mere

mechanical

mechanical action of receiving bread and wine at the hands of a parish Priest? He who believes them already needs not to be initiated by any such ceremony; and by what magick touch those simple elements are to convert the unbeliever, our author, who is master of so many secrets, has not condescended to explain. He will not pretend to impute the first spread of these doctrines in the infancy of the christian religion, or their revival at the reformation to any such means, since he imagines he can trace them in the New Testament. It is strange if that evidence which was powerful enough to introduce them where they were unknown, is not sufficient to uphold them where they are already professed and believed. At least the Test Act, it must be confessed, has yielded them no advantage, for they have been controverted with more acrimony, and admitted by a smaller number of persons, since that law was enacted, than in any period preceding.

Were the removal of this Test to overthrow the establishment itself, a consequence at the same time in the highest degree improbable, the articles of the church, if they are true, would remain unendangered, their evidence would continue unimpaired, an appeal to the inspired writings from which they profess to be derived would be open, the liberty of discussion would be admitted in as great an extent as at present; this difference only would occur, that an attachment to them would no longer be suspected of flowing from corrupt and sinister motives. They would cease to be with the clergy, the ladder of promotion, the cant of the pulpit, the ridicule of the schools. The futility of this or any other law, as a security to religious doctrines, may be discerned from this single reflection, that in the national church its own articles have for a length of time been either treated with contempt, or maintained with little sincerity, and no zeal; whilst amongst the Dissenters, where they have had no such aids, they have found a congenial soil, and continue to flourish with vigour.

On the political complexion of this Test, as it does not fall so properly within my present view, I shall content myself with remarking, that harmless as it may appear at first sight, it carries in it the seeds of all the persecutions and calamities which have ever been sustained on a religious account. It proscribes not an individual who has been convicted of a crime, but a whole party, as unfit to be trusted by the community to which they belong; and if this stigma can be justly fixed on any set of men, it ought not to stop *here, or any where*, short of the actual excision of those who are thus considered as rotten and incurable members of the political body. In annexing to religious speculation the idea of political default, the principle of this law would justify every excess of severity and rigour. If we are the persons it supposes, its indulgence is weak and contemptible; if we are of a different description, the nature of its pretensions is so extraordinary as to occasion serious alarm, and call aloud for its repeal. Mr. Clayton, indeed,

indeed, calls this, and similar laws, a restraint very prudently imposed upon those who dissent from the established religion *.

This restraint, however, is no less than a political annihilation, debarring them, though their talents were ever so splendid, from mingling in the councils, or possessing any share in the administration of their country. With that natural relish for absurdity, which characterizes this author, he imagines they have justly incurred this evil for dissenting from an *erroneous* religion.

He tells us, in the course of his sermon †, that the grand " principle of sepa-
" ration from the church lies in the un-
" worldly nature of our Saviour's king-
" dom." This reason for separation implies, that any attempt to blend worldly interests or policy with the constitution of a church, is improper; but how could this be done more effectually than by rendering the profession of its articles a preliminary step to every kind of civil pre-eminence. Yet this abuse, which in his own estima-

* Page 6. † Page 35.

tion

tion is so enormous as to form the great basis of separation, he wishes to perpetuate; and, all things considered, hopes " that " which is at rest will not be disturbed." In another part of his discourse*, he asks what temporalities has the church of Christ to expect? It is the mother of Harlots, which says, " I sit a queen, and shall see no sorrow." Would any one imagine this was the language of a man, who, in pleading for a Test Act, has rested the support of his creed on those very temporalities he affects so much to disdain, and has committed his religion to the arms of that mother of harlots to be reared and nourished! When speaking of the Test Act in the seventh page of his discourse, he thus expresses himself, " Surely the Cross of Christ ought not to be insulted by persons eager to press into the temple of Mammon." Who could treat it with more poignant severity than is couched in this declaration; yet this is the language of a person who desires its continuance. In truth, his re-

---

* Page 26.

presentations on this subject are pregnant with such contradictions, and rise above each other in so regular a gradation of absurdity as will not easily be conceived, and perhaps hath scarce ever been equalled. At the very outset of his sermon, he declares, " whenever the gospel is secularized " it is debased and misrepresented, and in " proportion to the quantity of foreign in- " fusions is the efficacy of this saving health " diminished." But human ingenuity would be at a loss to contrive a method of secularizing the gospel more completely, than by rendering it the common passport of all who aspire to civil distinctions. I am really weary of exposing the wild and extravagant incoherence of such a reasoner. From a man, who professing to be the apologist of his party, betrays its interests, and exhibits its most illustrious members to reproach, who himself a Dissenter, applauds the penalties which the hierarchy has inflicted as a " *prudent restraint*;" who, with the utmost poignance, censures a law which he solemnly invokes the legislature to perpetuate ;

petuate; and propofes to fecure the truths of religion, by the " prophanation of its " Sacraments *," by " debafing the Gof- " pel," and " infulting the Crofs;" any thing may be expected but confiftence and decency. When fuch an author affures us he was not impelled by vanity to publifh †, we may eafily give him credit; but he fhould remember, though it may be a virtue to fubdue vanity, it is bafe to extinguifh fhame. The tear which, he tells us, ftarted from the eyes of his audience, we will hope, for their honour, was an effufion of regret, natural to his friends, on hearing him deliver fentiments which they confidered as a difgrace to himfelf, and a calumny on his brethren. His affecting to pour contempt upon Dr. Price, whofe talents and character were revered by all parties, and to hold him up as the *corrupter* of the Diffenters, will not fail to awaken the indignation of every generous mind. Whether *they* were greater friends to their country, whofe pride and oppreffion fcattered the flames of

---

* See page 8.   † Page 6.

discord acrofs the atlantick, poured defolation into the colonies, difmembered the empire, and involved us in millions of debt; or the man, who, with a warning voice, endeavoured to avert thofe calamities, pofterity will decide.

He gives us a pompous enumeration * of the piety, learning, and talents of a large body of his brethren who concur with him in a difapprobation of the theological and political tenets of the Unitarians. The weaknefs of mingling them together has been fhown already; but if thefe great and eminent men, whom the world never heard of before, poffefs that zeal for their religion they pretend, let them meet their opponents on the open field of controverfy, where they may difplay their talents and prowefs to fomewhat more advantage than in *fkulking* behind a *confecrated altar*.

There are many particulars in the addrefs and fermon of an extraordinary complexion, which I have not noticed at all, as it was not my intention to follow the author ftep

* See page 6.

by

by step, but rather to collect his scattered representations into some leading points of view. For the same reason, I make no remarks on his barbarous imagery; or his stile, every where incoherent and incorrect, sometimes indecent, which cannot fail of disgusting every reader of taste. In a rude daubing peculiar to himself, where in ridicule of Dr. Priestley he has grouped together, a *foreigner*, a *ship*, and *cargo* of *drugs*, he has unfortunately sketched his own likeness, except in the circumstance of the *ship*, with tolerable accuracy; for, without the apology of having been *shipped* into England, he is certainly a *foreigner* in his native tongue, and his publication will be allowed to be a *drug*.

Had he known to apply the remark with which his address commences, on the utility of accommodating instruction to the exigence of times, he would have been aware, that this is not a season for drawing off the eyes of mankind from political objects. They were in fact never turned towards them with equal ardour, and we may venture to affirm, they will long continue to take that direction. An attention to the political aspect of the world, is not now the fruit of an idle curiosity, or the amusement of a dissipated and frivolous mind, but is awakened and kept alive by occurrences as various as they are extraordinary. There are times when the moral world seems to stand still; there are others when it seems impelled towards its goal, with an accelerated force. The present is a period more interesting, perhaps, than any which has been known, in the whole flight of time. The scenes of Providence thicken upon us so fast, and are shifted with so strange a rapidity, as if the great drama of the world were drawing to a close. Events have taken place, of late, and revolutions have been effected, which, had they been foretold a very few years ago, would have been viewed as visionary and extravagant, and their influence is yet far from being spent. Europe never presented such a spectacle before, and it is worthy of being contemplated, with the profoundest attention,

attention, by all its inhabitants. The empire of darkness and of despotism, has been smitten with a stroke which has sounded through the universe. When we see whole kingdoms, after reposing for centuries on the lap of their rulers, start from their slumber, the dignity of man rising up from depression, and tyrants trembling on their thrones, who can remain entirely indifferent, or fail to turn his eye towards a theatre so august and extraordinary. These are a kind of throes and struggles of nature, to which it would be a sullenness to refuse our sympathy. Old foundations are breaking up; new edifices are rearing. Institutions which have been long held in veneration, as the most sublime refinements of human wisdom and policy, which age hath cemented and confirmed, which power hath supported, which eloquence hath conspired to embellish and opulence to enrich, are falling fast into decay. New prospects are opening on every side, of such amazing variety and extent, as to stretch farther than
the

the eye of the most enlightened observer can reach.

Some beneficial effects appear to have taken place already, sufficient to nourish our most sanguine hope of benefits much more extensive. The mischief and folly of wars begin to be understood, and that mild and liberal system of policy adopted, which has ever indeed been the object of prayer to the humane and the devout, but has hitherto remained utterly unknown in the cabinets of princes. As the mind naturally yields to the impression of objects which it contemplates often, we need not wonder, if, amidst events so extraordinary, the human character itself should appear to be altering and improving apace. That fond attachment to ancient institutions, and blind submission to opinions already received, which has ever checked the growth of improvement, and drawn on the greatest benefactors of mankind danger, or neglect, is giving way to a spirit of bold and fearless investigation. Man seems to be becoming more erect and independant. He

leans

leans more on himself, less on his fellow-creatures. He begins to feel a consciousness in a higher degree of personal dignity, and is less enamoured of artificial distinctions. There is some hope of our beholding that simplicity and energy of character which marks his natural state, blended with the humanity, the elegance and improvement of polished society.

The events which have already taken place, and the further changes they forebode, will open to the contemplative of every character, innumerable sources of reflection. To the philosopher, they present many new and extraordinary facts, where his penetration will find ample scope in attempting to discover their cause, and to predict their effects. He will have an opportunity of viewing mankind in an interesting situation, and of tracing the progress of opinion through channels it has rarely flowed in before. The politician will feel his attention powerfully awakened, on seeing new maxims of policy introduced, new institutions established, and such a total alteration

teration in the ideas of a great part of the world, as will oblige him to study the art of government as it were afresh. The devout mind will behold in these momentous changes, the finger of God, and discerning in them the dawn of that glorious period, in which wars will cease, and antichristian tyranny shall fall, will adore that unerring wisdom, whose secret operation never fails to conduct all human affairs to their proper issue, and impels the great actors on that troubled theatre, to fulfil, when they least intend it, the counsels of heaven, and the predictions of its prophets.

FINIS.

A View of Revealed Religion;

A

SERMON,

PREACHED AT

THE ORDINATION

OF

THE REV. WILLIAM FIELD

OF WARWICK, JULY 12, 1790.

BY JOSEPH PRIESTLEY, LL.D. F.R.S.

WITH

A CHARGE,

Delivered at the fame Time,

BY THE REV. THOMAS BELSHAM.

———

BIRMINGHAM,
PRINTED BY *J. THOMPSON*;
AND SOLD BY J. JOHNSON, ST. PAUL'S CHURCH-YARD,
LONDON.

———

MDCCXC.

BT
127
A2P75

1053914

THE PREFACE.

THOUGH publications of the nature of *this* have seldom any extensive circulation, yet as some persons into whose hands it may fall, may want information concerning the idea of *ordination* that prevails among Dissenters, I shall observe that we (at least many of us) do not now mean by it the *giving of orders*, without which a person could not be considered as properly qualified to exercise the office of minister in a christian society. As all our societies are independent of each other, the members of each of them are, of course, the sole judges of the qualifications of the person whom they chuse to be their minister. Consequently their appointment is his proper *orders,* or *title to officiate* among them; and all that is done by the ministers who bear any part in what is usually called *the ordination service* (besides thereby virtually expressing their approbation of the choice of the congregation, and giving their minister the right hand of fellowship) is to recommend him and his labours to the divine blessing by prayer, and to give him and the people proper advice.

On this idea it is now customary with many Dissenters, especially those who are called Presbyterians, for the minister to discharge all the functions of his office, baptizing and administering the Lord's supper, as well as preaching

preaching and praying, before ordination, in order more effectually to remove the prejudices which still remain with many, founded on the idea that some powers are conferred on this occasion, powers which qualify him to do *after* this ceremony what he could not do *before*.

The proper *ordination service*, therefore, consists in the *prayer over the candidate*, and the *charge*. But the congregation, and also many strangers, being usually assembled on the occasion, and especially a number of ministers being present, it has been usual for one of them to deliver a discourse, or *sermon*, on some subject relating to christianity in general, or the ministry of it in particular; and instead of the particular *confession*

of

of faith, which was formerly required of all candidates for the miniftry (his foundnefs in which was then deemed effential) certain *queftions* are put to him, which lead him to give as much as he thinks proper of his views of chriftianity and the miniftry of it, and the motives and maxims of his own conduct, for the inftruction of the audience.

The ceremony of *impofition of hands*, which in primitive times accompanied the action of praying for a particular perfon, by which the apoftles communicated fpiritual gifts, and which was afterwards fuppofed to be neceffary to the conferring of proper qualifications for the gofpel miniftry, is now generally laid afide by us, fince we are confcious that we have

have nothing to impart, and wish not to encourage superstition.

Ordination being now no longer considered in the light of *conferring orders*, as in Epispocal, and the proper Presbyterian churches, many of the more liberal Dissenters neglect it altogether; thinking it to encourage superstition, and to keep up a mere *form* when the *substance* is wanting. But when the design of ordination, as above explained, is well understood, when the person ordained shall have performed every part of the ministerial duty before, as well as after, his ordination, though the name given to the service no longer suggests the idea that was formerly annexed to it, no superstition is encouraged. And since the con-

nexion

nexion between a minister and his congregation, and especially the first that he forms, is a very serious concern, there cannot, surely, be any impropriety, but on the contrary the greatest propriety, in making it an occasion of solemn prayer; and then exhortation or admonition, from a minister of greater age and experience, to one who has but lately entered upon the office, is particularly seasonable. I cannot help, therefore, expressing my wish, that some service, to which the name of *ordination* may well enough be given, may be kept up among us, at the same time that every precaution is taken to prevent superstition with respect to it.

J. PRIESTLEY.

Birmingham,
Nov. 1, 1790.

A

V I E W

OF

REVEALED RELIGION.

THE whole who had been at Athens frequently, and very much them of the great benefit derived from the knowledge of the — he does more especially in relation to this epistle to the Ephesians

A SERMON, &c.

—— That the God of our Lord Jesus Christ, the Father of glory, may give unto you the spirit of wisdom and revelation, in the knowledge of him; the eyes of your understanding being enlightened; that ye may know what is the hope of his calling, and what the riches of the glory of his inheritance in the saints, and what is the exceeding greatness of his power, to us-ward who believe, according to the working of his mighty power, which he wrought in Christ, when he raised him from the dead.

EPHES. i. 17—20.

THE apostle, writing to those who had lately been heathens, frequently, and very properly, reminds them of the great benefit they derived from the knowledge of the gospel. This he does more especially in the introduction to this epistle to the Ephesians.

Ephesians. It is indeed, of great importance that our minds should always be impressed with a sense of what we owe to the fountain of all good in this most important respect, especially as, having never ourselves seen, or known, much of heathenism, we are too apt to think less of the happiness of our emancipation from it. And as we are now assembled for the purpose of recommending to the divine blessing a fellow labourer in the work of the christian ministry, I shall take the opportunity of bringing to the recollection of this christian assembly, and of myself, the several particulars of which the knowledge we derive from revelation, and more especially from christianity, consists.

But I shall first consider the propriety of having recourse to any measures whatever on the part of the Divine Being, farther than the natural means that he had employed for the moral improvement of mankind.

That

That the Divine Being has really made provision for promoting the virtue and happiness of men in the constitution of nature and of the world, is not to be denied. There are numberless particulars in the make of our bodies, and in the faculties of our minds, which, if attended to, will teach us that vice and wickedness (consisting in the excessive and irregular indulgence of our passions) is hurtful to man; that it tends to debase our natures, and subjects us to pain and anguish; and that if we would live in the greatest dignity and happiness, we must live in the habitual practice of all virtue. Some will, therefore, ask, Is not nature alone a sufficient guide to virtue and happiness? and may not men, by these helps, and the proper use of the *reason* with which they are endued, be their own instructors? Why might not mankind have been left to themselves, when their own reason, assisted by observation and experience, would teach them to correct their vices, and improve their natures to the utmost?

and when the Divine Being had done thus much for us, what occasion was there for his doing any thing more?

In replying to this, it must be acknowledged that, if men would make the most of their reason, and conscientiously obey all its dictates, it would be a sufficient director in the conduct of life. But what must we say if, from whatever cause, and through whatever foreign influence, men become indisposed to make this right use of their reason, and especially if they be not sufficiently apprized of all the consequences of their conduct; and if, in that state of ignorance and darkness, they want stronger *motives* than will ever occur to themselves, to the practice of universal virtue. In these circumstances it was surely highly expedient that the great parent and friend of mankind should interpose, to apprize them of these consequences, that he should send proper persons, duly authorized, to engage their attention, and thus to inform their judgment, interest their affections, and direct their conduct.

I must

I muſt farther obſerve, in anſwer to thoſe who object to the ſcheme of ſuch *occaſional interpoſitions*, and who are ſtruck with the idea of the ſuperior dignity of an abſolutely uninterrupted operation of the *eſtabliſhed laws*, that we are not at liberty to ſuppoſe either *man*, or *the world*, to be conſtituted differently from what they are; becauſe we are no proper judges of ſuch different arrangements of things and their conſequences. And conſidering how men are actually conſtituted, we may ſafely conclude that if it was at all neceſſary (as we cannot but ſuppoſe it to be) that ſuch beings as we are ſhould keep up an *attention* to their maker, this great end will be better anſwered by his maintaining ſome viſible intercourſe with them, than by a rigorous adherence to any original conſtitution of things whatever, while himſelf was kept out of view.

The bulk of mankind (and by this we are to judge) do not naturally inquire into the cauſe of what they ſee to be *conſtant* and *invariable*. They ſee, for example, the fun to rife and fet, and all the changes of the feafons to take place, without ever reflecting on their author, or final caufe, or at leaft acquiefcing in any lame account of them, fo that fomething out of the common courfe of nature was neceffary to arreft their attention, and lead them to think of the author of nature, of what they fee and experience every day.

The authors of the Greek and Roman theology never went farther in their fpeculations than the *vifible univerfe*. They had gods in great abundance, but imagined the world to be more antient than them all; and the great object of the moft antient idolatry were the fun, moon, and ftars, the earth, and other parts of *nature*, having never imagined that thefe had any author.

Befides, in order that man may keep up an idea of God, as a *perfon*, a being with whom they have to do, as the infpector and judge of their conduct, it feems neceffary that there fhould be on his part
fome

some *personal acts*, such as promulgating laws, sending messengers, expressing his pleasure or displeasure at their conduct, and the like. Without something of this kind, the course of nature, though bearing infinite marks of intelligence, might never suggest the idea of an *intelligent person*, the proper object of prayer, a lawgiver, and a judge.

We clearly see this in the case of numbers who, disbelieving revelation, do at this day, seriously maintain that there is no intelligent principle in the universe, besides the visible works of nature. They, therefore, do not admit what we may call the *personality of the supreme cause of all*; and without this there will never be any such thing as piety towards God, as a Being whom we conceive to be ever present with us, as the inspector and the judge of our conduct. These persons never pray.

For want of this the best of the heathens were intirely destitute of that most essential branch of virtue. And without an habitual regard to God, as our common parent, there is no sufficient foundation for the duties we owe to his offspring, or even the duties that respect ourselves. Where there is no proper *lawgiver*, there can be no proper *law*. Without a proper regard to God in all our ways, our minds would be liable to be disturbed and unhinged by the events of life, and we should more especially find ourselves destitute of power to carry us through severe trials and sufferings in the cause of truth and a good conscience. But an habitual respect to the being, the presence, and the providence of God, extending through this life and the next, is abundantly sufficient for all these purposes. It was therefore, most truly said by our Lord, *No man cometh to the Father but by me*, or, as we may interpret it, *revealed religion* is the only

foundation

foundation of what is termed *natural religion*.

It is not only on the authority of the moſt probable *reaſons*, but on the evidence of the moſt indiſputable *facts*, that we aſſert the neceſſity of extraordinary interpoſitions on the part of the Divine Being, to engage the attention of mankind to himſelf, in order to reform the world, and reſtore the practice of virtue among men. We ſee in hiſtory how groſsly ignorant the heathen world remained of the nature and perfections of God, and of the purity of his worſhip, and how loſt they were to a juſt ſenſe of piety and virtue, while they were ſuffered to continue without ſupernatural revelation. And from the length of time in which the wiſeſt and moſt poliſhed nations continued in this ſtate of ignorance and corruption, it was manifeſt that natural means were not ſufficient to enlighten their minds, and reform their conduct. Theſe, as we are authorized

authorized to say, had been long tried without effect. For while arts and sciences were cultivated, and brought to a considerable degree of perfection, religious notions, and religious rites, became, if possible, more absurd. For after the worship of the sun, moon, and stars (which was the original idolatry of mankind, and continued to be that of the more barbarous part of the world) the polished Egyptians and Greeks added that of dead men. And how deplorable, in a moral respect, is the state of those parts of the world to which the knowledge of christianity has not reached, or in which its glorious and salutary light is extinguished.

It was therefore a measure highly worthy of the wisdom and goodness of almighty God, in order to accomplish his gracious design of raising men to a state of glory and happiness, to appoint some persons to be, as it were, his embassadors to the world lying in darkness and wickedness, ednefs, to inftruct them in the truths relating to their moft important concerns, and to lay before them, with plainnefs and energy, the proper motives for reforming their conduct; and it was neceffary that, for this purpofe, thefe perfons fhould come with authority, bearing evident tokens of a divine miffion, by the working of *miracles*, or fuch works as men might be fatisfied could not be performed without God, the author of nature, and who alone can control its laws, being with them.

With this view, if any hiftory be credible, the Divine Being has actually commiffioned various perfons to communicate his will to mankind, and efpecially to warn them of the future confequences of their evil conduct. Thefe perfons were chiefly of the nation of the Jews; and the object of their miffions was to inftruct their countrymen in the firft inftance, and then other nations who had

intercourfe

intercourſe with them, in the fundamental principles of true religion, in order to guard them againſt the abominable vices and extravagancies to which idolatry naturally led them. In like manner was Jeſus Chriſt (of the ſame nation of the Jews) commiſſioned to bring the laſt and moſt complete revelation of the will of God to man; ſo that nothing now remains to be done on the part of God for the moral inſtruction and reformation of the world.

What it is that God has by theſe repeated revelations done for mankind, and eſpecially by Jeſus Chriſt, I ſhall now proceed to ſpecify. But I muſt farther premiſe, that the great and ultimate object of the miſſion of Chriſt was not at all different from that of the preceding prophets. According to his own repreſentation, in the inſtructive parable of the vineyard let out to huſbandmen, God firſt ſent *ſervants* to them, to receive the fruits

fruits of the vineyard, and laſt of all, with the ſame general view, he ſent his *ſon*, or a perſon ſo much more diſtinguiſhed, as to be entitled to that peculiar appellation, though he was of *the ſame nature* with them, *in all things like unto his brethren.*

1. By theſe extraordinary interpoſitions we have been inſtructed in the nature, perfections, and moral government of God, and the rule of human duty; a knowledge of a very important nature, and which mankind, after having been inſtructed in it, by *becoming vain in their imaginations*, had loſt. This knowledge we find in Moſes and all the prophets. There we find that God is one, that he made and governs the world, that he is every where preſent, obſerving the conduct of men, that he is merciful to the penitent, but will puniſh the obſtinately wicked. We are alſo taught in revelation how the one true God is to be worſhipped in the moſt acceptable manner,

ner, viz. *in spirit and in truth*, by purity of heart, and uprightnefs of life. According to Chrift, the two great commandments, which include all the reft, are the love of God and of our fellow-creatures.

Thus was laid the foundation of all acceptable worfhip, and right conduct in life, and thus were the minds of men freed from a flavifh and debafing fuperftition, which had taught them to feek to pleafe God by other things than true goodnefs of heart and life, and had encouraged them to continue in the practice of vice, by trufting to vain compenfations and atonements. This was one of the moft important fervices that could be rendered to religion, and to mankind; as there is nothing to which they appear to be more prone than *fuperftition*, or unworthy notions of God, and confequently wrong methods of feeking to pleafe him.

Beginning with thefe leading principles, did our Lord, following the example of the

the prophets who had preceded him, go on to inſtruct mankind in every uſeful principle of religion, concealing from them nothing that could in any reſpect influence their practice. And this, we clearly ſee, had the moſt direct tendency to promote the great ſcheme of our redemption, or deliverance from vice and miſery. For before men can be reclaimed from vicious courſes, they muſt be convinced of the evil of them. They muſt be ſhewn againſt how great a Being they are offending, and be informed what it is that will recommend them to his favour. Such knowledge as this is, in its own nature, neceſſary to all virtuous and religious practice. The judgment, or underſtanding, muſt firſt be enlightened, before the will can be renewed, the affections regulated, and the conducted reformed; as, in all caſes, a thing muſt be *underſtood*, before it can be *practiſed*.

This excellent moral inſtruction was not, however, as I have ſaid already, peculiar to Chrift. He did not pretend to teach men any thing *new* on thefe fubjects. He only explained and enforced what had long before been taught by Mofes and the prophets. But many of thefe excellent and moft important moral precepts had been perverted, and the folid duties of piety, benevolence, and all virtue, had been made to give place to a moft debafing and mifchievous fuperftition. The fame, indeed, has been the cafe with the moral precepts of chriftianity itfelf; fo that there will always be great reafon to caution men on this head, fo prone are they to the indulgence of their appetites and paffions, and fo willing to find fome fubftitute for moral virtue, if they can.

Chrift did not teach any thing new concerning God, or the maxims of his government, becaufe thefe things were fufficiently known to the Jews, and explained in their fcriptures. The great doctrine of the *divine unity* was well underftood, and taken for granted, by all the

the nation of the Jews. That there is *one God*, and there is *no other than he*, and that *to worship him with the heart, is better than all whole burnt-offerings and sacrifice*, was a reply of a Jewish scribe to our Saviour, and which met with his perfect approbation.

Least of all had he any occasion to inform them that the Divine Being, the God and Father of all, as well as his own God and Father, was placable to his penitent creatures. This most necessary of all doctrines had been most clearly taught by Moses and all the prophets; so that nothing farther remained to be said on the subject. By Moses the Divine Being solemnly proclaimed himself to be *a God merciful and gracious, long-suffering, abundant in mercy, goodness, and truth, forgiving iniquity, transgression, and sin.* All the prophets exhorted to repentance on the same principle. *Return unto me, and I will return unto you,* is the constant burden of their preaching. Indeed, without this all exhortation to repentance would be in vain.

That Chrift was himfelf, by his death and fufferings, the means of reconciling men to God, and of making it to be confiftent with his juftice to pardon the truly penitent, is a doctrine for which there is no countenance either in the difcourfes of our Lord, or the writings of the apoftles. They all took it for granted, that all that was neceffary to be done was to reconcile finful man to God, not to reconcile God to man. In the fine parable of the prodigal fon, Chrift informs us that God, our true and affectionate Father, is ready to receive all his offending and penitent children, as it were, with open arms, without any interceffion of others, or any atonement whatever. Through the whole of the fcriptures God is reprefented as forgiving fin *freely*, and for *his mercy's*, or *his name's fake only*.

2. To give the greater weight to their inftructions, all the prophets of God, with fome few exceptions, exemplified them by their own conduct.

But

But the benefit we derive from the example of good men recorded in the fcriptures is only incidental, and is not to be confidered as any proper part of the fcheme of revelation. Nay the examples of bad men, equally recorded in the fcriptures, or in other authentic hiftories, may fometimes be of as much ufe to us as that of good men. Since, however, as chriftians, we profefs to be, and are exhorted to be, in a more efpecial manner followers of Chrift, I fhall make a few obfervations with refpect to this fubject.

Now the example of Chrift, like that of other good men, can only be of partial and occafional ufe to us. In a great variety of the moft trying fituations our Lord was never placed, fo that in thofe cafes his life cannot furnifh any pattern for us. It is his general temper and character that we are to attend to, and an attention to this may be of great ufe to us, even in fituations in which he himfelf was never placed. What were moft con-

fpicuous

spicuous in him were the virtues of meekness, humility, heavenly-mindedness, and an intire devotedness to the will of God, in suffering as well as in doing; and with these dispositions we shall in no particular case act wrong.

In obedience to the will of God, and to answer the great designs of his providence, he gave up his innocent life to the malice of his enemies, who put him to death in the most cruel and ignominious manner, in this, as well as in other things leaving us an example that we should follow his steps. *Forasmuch as Christ suffered in the flesh, we must arm ourselves*, as Peter says, *with the same mind. Because he laid down his life for us, we ought also*, as John says, *to lay down our lives for the brethren*; that is, we ought to serve mankind, at the hazard of every thing dear to us in life, and even of life itself.

Our Lord's great heroism in suffering and dying as he did, will be more admired

mired the more we confider the circumftances of it, efpecially his extreme fenfibility. That a man whofe bodily frame was capable of fuffering fo much as his did under the mere *apprehenfion* of his approaching death, fhould, nothwithftanding this, die with fuch noble and calm fortitude, and with fuch fentiments of piety and benevolence even to his enemies, is, indeed, wonderful. There is alfo fomething peculiarly trying in being the *firft* to fuffer in any caufe. In bearing, however, not only pain, but hardfhips of various kinds, (fome of them more trying than any kind of violent death) and bearing them alfo with a truly chriftian fpirit, it is for the honour of chriftianity, and confequently of Chrift, to fay that many of the martyrs have not fallen fhort of the pattern fet them.

As to the more common infirmities of human nature, fuch as the indulgence of fenfual appetites and paffions, we cannot fuppofe that the temptation to tranfgrefs would be much felt by a perfon of his exalted character, and great expectations, and with a violent death in immediate prospect. There is, therefore, nothing very extraordinary, though highly worthy of our imitation, in this part of our Saviour's conduct.

I shall close this head with observing that, in all cases in which the example of *men* cannot be recommended, that of the ever blessed *God* is proposed to us in the scriptures. For we are exhorted to *be perfect as our Father who is in heaven is perfect*. This precept has the advantage of being an unerring rule of conduct. It will prevent our acquiescing in any limited degree of moral excellence; and recourse may be had to it with great advantage in those cases in which the supremacy of the Divine Being, and his infinite knowledge (by which he ever sees the most distant consequences of things, and by which he can bring good out of all evil) does not necessarily make the rule of *his* conduct different from that of *ours*.

3. In

3. In order to reform the world, and thereby raise men to a state of future glory and happiness, God has by Jesus Christ, in a more especial manner, revealed to them the knowledge of a future state of rewards and punishments, as supplying the most effectual motive to the practice of virtue. This is, indeed, the distinguishing excellence of the gospel. By this gospel *life and immortality are fully brought to light*, as it affords a more satisfactory evidence of a resurrection to a future and immortal life than had been given to the world before, so as to establish the belief of this most important of all truths to the end of time. This great end Christ effected, not only by preaching the doctrine with authority from God, evidenced by miracles, even such as raising the dead to life, but by being himself an example of what he announced to others; having submitted to die in the most public and indisputable manner, and having been raised to life, to the complete satisfaction

of

of a sufficient number of the most competent witnesses.

Had mankind, in a body, been asked what evidence they required for a doctrine so important and interesting to them, they could not have demanded more than was actually given them, viz. that the great preacher of the doctrine should, in his own person, afford them an example of its truth, by dying and rising again within a limited time.

This was no new doctrine to the Jews. The great body of that nation were then, and are to this day, fully persuaded of it. This must, in my opinion, have arisen from some very early revelation from God on the subject, but probably prior to the writing of the books of Moses; whatever difficulty we may now find in accounting for the remarkable silence concerning a doctrine of so much importance in his writings, as well as those of the Old Testament

tament in general. Had this great revelation been made to Mofes himfelf, or to any of the fubfequent prophets, we could not but have heard of it. But having been made known probably to our firft parents, and, though it was loft in other nations, having been always retained by the Jews, there was the lefs occafion for any mention of it in books defigned for their peculiar ufe. But what was well known to the Jews would be *good tidings of great joy* to the Gentile world, which was ignorant of it.

When *the fulnefs of time was come,* that God thought proper to manifeft his paternal regards to all his offspring of mankind, it was highly proper that, as the original record of this great doctrine of a refurrection was then loft, it fhould be renewed; that fo no reafonable doubt might remain concerning it; and this was completely effected by the refurrection of Chrift, who likewife brought it into view in all his difcourfes. For he did not, like Mofes,

Moses, give his disciples any expectation of happiness in this life, but only at the resurrection of the just; and to this *great hope that was set before them*, he taught them chearfully to sacrifice all their interests here, and even life itself; assuring them that they who should lose their lives for the sake of the gospel, would receive them again, with infinite advantage, in the world to come. It was his express declaration, that his kingdom was not of this world, and he enjoined all his followers to *lay up their treasure in heaven*. We also learn from the apostle that we are to *walk by faith and not by sight*, since the *things that are seen are temporary, but the things that are unseen are eternal*.

When God had by this means imparted to mankind this most important information concerning himself and his moral government, concerning their duty here, and their expectations hereafter, nothing more was requisite in order completely to effect his great design, the reformation of of the world, and the preparation of men for that future happy ſtate which is announced to us in the goſpel. For with theſe helps, the rational nature that God had originally given to man was ſufficient, without any ſupernatural operation upon their minds, to their reſtoration to his favour and their future happineſs. The hiſtorical evidence that we now have of the miracles, the death, and reſurrection of Chriſt, is of itſelf ſufficient to produce *chriſtian faith*, or a firm belief of the great facts on which chriſtianity reſts; and this faith, or belief, is ſufficient to induce men to reform their conduct, and to fit them, by a life of virtue here, for a ſtate of happineſs hereafter.

Accordingly, no farther help than this is ever promiſed to us in the goſpel. Like good ſeed, in our Saviour's moſt inſtructive parable, it is ſcattered promiſcuouſly on all kinds of ſoil; but nothing is done to the ſoil itſelf, and therefore it brings forth much fruit, or none at all, juſt as the

the minds of men were previously disposed to receive it. The *gift of the spirit*, of which we read, always means some *miraculous power*, calculated for the confirmation of the gospel in the early ages only. We are taught, indeed, to pray to God to be led into, and to be kept in, the ways of truth and virtue. But we are also taught to pray for our daily bread; and as our daily bread is not given to us without our own labour, so likewise good dispositions of mind are only to be acquired by the use of proper means; though both the means, and the power of using them, being from God, it is right to ascribe all to him, to pray to him for every blessing, temporal or spiritual, and to thank him for all of them alike.

As a practical improvement of this doctrine, I shall observe (1.) that from it we may infer the dignity of human nature; man being a creature the most distinguished by his great creator among his works here below, in that we are the

proper

proper subjects of his moral government, and fit heirs of immortality. This implies that we are capable of unlimited improvement; and what we see of man in this life makes this probable. We see no bounds to increasing knowledge and ripening virtue, though we, and all created beings, shall ever fall infinitely short of the perfection of the supreme Being, who is, and ever will be, alone, the *absolutely good*.

Let us, then, my brethren, with all humility and gratitude to God, for every thing that we have, or are, respect ourselves, as so greatly distinguished by the author of all excellence, and not carelessly and wickedly abandon the glorious prospects that are set before us. For a beggar in our streets to reject the offer of a kingdom, would not be more preposterous. We can hardly form an idea of greater depravity of mind than for a man seriously to prefer utter annihilation to that immortality which is brought to light

light by the gospel, and to maintain that the great and extensive views it opens to us do not tend to enlarge and exalt the mind, and qualify men to act with more dignity, generosity, and integrity, as well as true piety, in this life, in consequence of being taught that the connexions and habits which we form here below, will be continued beyond the grave, where we shall again find ourselves under the government of the same God, and be again happy in our subjection to him, and in our renewed intercourse with each other to all eternity. To maintain, as some have done, that this christian doctrine of a future state has any hurtful tendency, appears to me to argue such depravity of mind, as can only be produced by gross vices, such as make men secretly wish that it may not be true. Thousands have found that the firm belief of it tends to make men *purify themselves even as God is pure.*

2. Let

2. Let us learn from this doctrine to cherish a sense of the great blessings of christianity, as the only means of giving men this glorious prospect, and preparing them for future happiness. For that any of the human race will survive the grave nature gives us no reason to expect.

Christians would have a much higher sense of the value of the gospel, if they had not forgotten what heathenism was. That such vices as the heathens were addicted to, some of them too abominable and horrid to be mentioned in such a place as this, should have been encouraged by any thing that ever bore the name of *religion*, and even should have been practiced as *religious rites*, which recommend men to the object of their worship, would not now be credible, did not the most authentic history remain as an indisputable evidence of the facts. Let us then bless God for the gospel, which brings us from darkness to light, from vice to virtue,

from

from death to immortaltty; and let us do every thing in our power to extend the knowledge and the bleffings of it to all the human race. More efpecially, as a means to the great end, let us exert ourfelves to purify it from thofe corruptions which both defeat the great defign of it, and prevent its reception among Jews, Mahometans, and heathens. This fatal tendency has every thing that, in any degree, renders it lefs amiable, or lefs credible; and nothing does this more than any infringement of the great doctrine of the *unity of God*, and the equity of his government.

3. All that I have reprefented having been done for us, the beft inftructions having been given us for a virtuous life, exemplified by the lives of holy men, prophets, and Jefus Chrift; having had the moft fatisfactory evidence given us of a future ftate of retribution after death, nothing more could have been done to
induce

induce men to abandon a courfe of vice, and to live in fuch a manner as to fecure a happy immortality. If the nature of *virtue*, and of *man*, be confidered, it will be evident that nothing more could have been done for us. The *will* cannot be forced. It can only be determined by proper motives. God requires that we fhould give him our *hearts*, which can only be engaged by the force of perfuafion.

As far, therefore, as it became the Divine Being to interpofe, nothing has been left untried to reform the world. If then, notwithftanding all thefe meafures for our good, we continue difobedient, and addicted to vice, may not the Divine Being with the greateft propriety fpeak of us as of the children of Ifrael of old. " What " could I have done to my vineyard more " than I have done; neverthelefs when, I " looked that it fhould bring forth grapes, " it brought forth wild grapes."

We cannot think that, after all this that has been done for us, we are at liberty to neglect and flight it, and that God will take no notice of our difobedience and perverfenefs. No, our fins under the difpenfation of the gofpel are attended with every aggravation that can heighten their guilt, and increafe our condemnation. As the apoftle fays, *which way can we come off, or efcape, if we neglect fo great falvation.* Let it not be our condemnation, that *light is come into the world, but that we loved darknefs rather than light, becaufe our deeds were evil.*

We who profefs what we wifh to be confidered as *rational chriftianity*, have leaft of all any juft excufe for a deficiency in that temper, and a want of thofe good works, which our religion requires. We, depending upon the free mercy of God to the penitent, reject the idea of being faved by any righteoufnefs that is not our own. We believe that no man can obey the laws

laws of God for another, or suffer the punishment due to the crimes of another; and we disclaim the belief of any thing whatever standing in the place of moral virtue. We believe the gospel both to contain a sufficient rule of life, and also sufficient motives to the observance of it.

As therefore, my brethren, we not only *name the name of Christ*, and profess ourselves to be his disciples, but think that we profess it in greater purity than many others, let us give proof of it by departing farther from all iniquity, and by being *a peculiar people zealous of good works*. If this be not our resolution, and steady uniform conduct, there is not a nation under heaven that will not rise up against us, and condemn us, at the last day. For no people ever enjoyed greater advantages than we do. If they neglect their advantages, which are inferior to ours, their condemnation will be proportionably less. But if they improve them, while we neglect ours, double will be their recompence,

pence, and double will be our condemnation. May we all seriously consider these things, *the things that relate to our everlasting peace and welfare, before they be for ever hid from our eyes.*

END OF THE SERMON.

Mr. BELSHAM's

CHARGE.

A

CHARGE

ADDRESSED TO

THE REV. WILLIAM FIELD.

THE hints of advice, Sir, which I shall upon this occasion submit to your consideration, will take their rise chiefly from that declaration of St. Paul, in which, in a few comprehensive words, he exhibits his own character, and that of every faithful minister of the gospel.

> 2 Cor. ii. 17. *For we are not as many which corrupt the word of God: but as of sincerity, but as of God, in the sight of God, speak we in Christ.*

I shall

I shall not detain you at present, with illustrating the connexion in which the words of the text are introduced: it is sufficient for my purpose, to observe that they appear to express in the judgment of St. Paul, a summary of the duties of the christian minister, and of the temper and spirit by which he ought to be actuated in the discharge of his office, and without which, whatever his abilities and attainments may be, he will prove but as *the sounding brass, or the tinkling cymbal*, and cannot rationally expect either honour, comfort, or success.

In the first place, the great duty of a christian minister is to *speak in Christ*.

You well know, Sir, that the apostle Paul, amidst the variety of engagements which continually crouded upon him, had not much time to spare for epistolary correspondence; so that when he was under a necessity of writing to his particular friends, or to christian societies, he studied

a degree

a degree of brevity which not unfrequently borders upon obscurity, and he often comprizes a multitude of ideas in very few words. To *speak in Christ* is an elliptical expression by which we are then to understand (as I presume no person at all conversant with this apostle's writings will dispute) teaching the doctrine of Christ, that doctrine which had been *revealed to St. Paul by Christ**, the doctrine which Christ himself had preached, which he had confirmed by his miracles, which he had sealed with his blood, and which he had commissioned this eminent apostle, who from a furious persecutor had been transformed into a zealous advocate for truth and righteousness, to diffuse through the world, both among Jews and Gentiles.†

In this respect christian ministers are the true successors of the apostles; and

* Gal. i. 12.   † Acts xxvi. 17, 18.

though they profefs not to have received either their inftructions, or their call, from fuch high authority, nor to challenge that implicit regard to their meffage which the apoftles often claimed, and to which they were juftly entitled, in confequence of the extent and accuracy of their views of chriftian doctrine, the authority which they received from Chrift, the gift of the Holy Spirit, and the miraculous powers with which they were furnifhed; yet it is their great duty, the honour and the privilege of their office, to publifh what they apprehend to be the true doctrine of Chrift, as the reprefentatives of their great mafter, to addrefs men in his name, to teach what he taught, and, as *the embaffadors of Chrift, to befeech them in Chrift's ftead to be reconciled to God**.

Upon this head it were eafy to enlarge, and to multiply directions; but I forbear. Your own heart, Sir, will inftruct

* 2 Cor. v. 20.

you

you in your duty, and will supply you with the best motives to the faithful diligent performance of it. But one hint I must take leave to suggest, viz. that it is an object of the highest importance to the interest of truth and piety, that a minister should be particularly attentive to the rising generation, and should spare no pains to instil into the young and susceptible mind, just and pleasing apprehensions of religious truth. That the idea of God may be one of the earliest impressions upon the understanding; that from the first moment when children learn to lisp his name, they may think of him with delight, as their best and kindest friend, and may associate the most pleasing sentiments with the duties they owe to God. A filial spirit is what God requires; it is that fragrant incense which ought to perfume every sacrifice. It is that alone which renders every duty pleasant in the performance, and acceptable to God. The sooner this spirit is infused the better: and this can only be
accomplished

accomplished by exhibiting to young people the most pleasing, which are at the same time the most rational and beneficial, views of the supreme Being. Of those who are grown old in wickedness there is very little hope.

If you can check the career of folly, if you can moderate the excesses of vice, if you can effect some external reformation; this is all that in ordinary cases you can reasonably expect. But that *which has long been crooked cannot easily be made straight**. *The Ethiopian cannot change his skin, nor the leopard his spots*†. If false and gloomy thoughts of God and his government have taken early possession of the mind, if by length of time and force of habit, they have entwined themselves about the fibres of the heart, and have associated themselves with every devotional sentiment, it is in vain to hope that the baneful and deep-rooted prejudice will yield to the

* Ecclef. i. 15.   † Jer. xiii. 23.

THE CHARGE. 47

gentle influence of calm and fober argument. Death, the *great teacher*, can alone emancipate the underftanding, and eradicate thofe hard injurious thoughts of the moft amiable and beneficent of Beings, which embitter human life, and pervert to dejection and defpondency thofe exercifes of piety which to an enlightened and upright mind, are an inexhauftible fource of confolation and pleafure. But if here and there an inftance fhould occur of perfons who in advanced age poffefs leifure, inclination, and ftrength of mind, to examine into the foundation of their prejudices, and to correct their unhappy errors concerning the Supreme Being, the feelings will not eafily, perhaps never entirely, follow the dictates of the underftanding; and when the attention is diverted to a different object, the old affociations and modes of thinking and feeling will return again, as though the judgment had never been convinced.

It is, then, an object of unfpeakable importance not only that young people
fhould

should be trained up to the practice of religion, but that their religious principles should be rightly formed; that they should be kept from all those views of God, and his government, and of the duties he requires, which would damp the innocent chearfulness of the mind, would inspire it with terror, and produce a servile and reluctant homage, so opposite to that filial spirit, that chearful obedience, which is most acceptable to God. It is very desirable that young persons should never recollect the time when they were not firm believers in the existence and goodness of God, when they did not think of him with sentiments of reverence and affection, when they did not rejoice in his protection, and government, and when they did not consider obedience to God as a privilege, as well as a duty.

And here, Sir, in my apprehension, a minister's chief business and pleasure lies. Here he is called upon to exert his most valuable talents with the fairest prospect of success, viz. in fixing the best impressions

pressions upon the tender minds of the younger part of his society, and that by means of private instruction as well as by public addresses. And give me leave to hint an observation of the utmost moment to the success of your ministry, that the most important duties of the sacred office, are not those which are performed in public. I am, indeed, persuaded that the public preaching of the gospel is highly useful, and that without it the world would be much more ignorant and vicious than it now is. I admire the orator who can exhibit the interesting doctrines, and the essential duties of christianity in clear, elegant, and harmonious language; who can support them by the most cogent arguments, who can enforce them by the most engaging motives, who can command attention, and can reach the heart by graceful elocution, united with manly sense, and with that genuine pathos which results from a firm conviction of the truth and importance of his subject, and from an earnest desire to be useful to his hearers

THE CHARGE.

hearers in their moſt important concerns, I cordially wiſh him ſuccefs. And multitudes, no doubt, are enlightened, and edified, and ſaved by his miniſtry. But yet, I am perſuaded that it is the *ſtill ſmall voice* of private inſtruction, of prudent advice, of friendly admonition, of ſalutary reproof, of tender ſymapthy, and of chriſtian conſolation, which is uſually found moſt efficacious to open the underſtanding, and to meliorate the heart. The wiſe and vigilant, and faithful miniſter, therefore, will be *inſtant in ſeaſon, and out of ſeaſon*, and will diligently ſeek after, and never willingly let ſlip, any favourable opportunity of promoting the cauſe of truth, and the intereſt of religion.

I now proceed, ſecondly, To illuſtrate that temper and ſpirit by which the apoſtle was animated, and which he inſinuates to be neceſſary to form the character of a chriſtian miniſter. *We are not as many who corrupt the word of God, but as of ſincerity, but as of God, in the ſight of God ſpeak we in Chriſt.*

In

In the first place, a christian minister is to be very careful that he doth not, as many do, corrupt the word of God.

You need not, Sir, to be informed that the expression *, in the original, signifies to debase generous liquors by impure mixtures for the fake of gain. And the apostle means to declare, that he did not adulterate the pure doctrine of Christ by the mixture of any foreign or inferior principles, as many at that time did. He particularly alludes to the judaizing zealots, who blended the ceremonies of the Mosaic ritual, and the absurdities, and burdens, of Pharisaic tradition, with the doctrine of Christ, and represented them as essential to salvation. The apostle could truly say that he did not, in this, nor in any other way, adulterate the word of God. For he knew it perfectly. He had learned it by express *revelation from Christ*†. Nor would he presume to violate the sacred depositum.

* Καπηλευοντες. † Gal. i. 12.

But what minister of the gospel will *now* presume to affirm that he in particular doth never corrupt the word of God? That the doctrine which *he* teaches, is the genuine, unmingled, undebased doctrine of Christ? That the christian religion has been sullied by grievous corruptions, is what we are all ready to acknowledge; that it is the duty of ministers to teach the word of God purified, as far as possible, from the dross of human inventions, none will deny. But where is the touchstone of truth, the key of knowledge to be found? Who will take off from our eyes the bandage of ignorance and prejudice? Who will direct us to the abode of truth, or discover to us the heavenly stranger? I am happy in the persuasion, that the world, under the benign influence of the gospel, and the government of perfect wisdom and goodness, is proceeding to a better state. All things are advancing to perfection by a gradual, but continually accelerated progress, and the time is approaching, when truth will reveal her radiant form to every upright inquisitive

inquisitive mind. Yes, my heart triumphs in the prospect of that glorious state of things, which the pen of prophecy has delineated in the fairest colours, when truth and peace shall visit this world, and the pure doctrine of Christ, by its intrinsic energy, and the superintending providence of God, shall purge itself thoroughly from all the feculence of error, and shall diffuse its saving beams throughout the world. The happy day is even now beginning to dawn. The rays of truth already penetrate the gloom, and error, ignorance, and superstition are gradually vanishing before it. The darkness is passed, and the true light now begins to shine. Happy they who will hereafter be witnesses to its meridian splendour. Happy we, my brethren, if like the venerable patriarch, we can look forward to the *day of Christ**. This is our best solace amidst the struggles to which an honest zeal for truth, and the difficulties to which a laborious, patient,

---

* John viii. 56.

serious

serious enquiry after it, and an honest open profession of it, will *now* sometimes expose us. But, in the mean time, we must esteem it our honour, if we are employed as instruments in promoting this glorious cause, either by our labours, or by our sufferings.

It is your duty then, Sir, if you are desirous of keeping clear of the charge of *corrupting* the word of God, to study the scriptures with care and diligence; to divest your mind as far as possible of every prejudice; to aim at nothing but truth; to search after the genuine sense of the sacred writers, without warping it to support a favourite system; never to think that you have learned enough, nor to be ashamed of acknowledging an error; ever to keep your mind open to conviction, and to be thankful for every degree of information, from whatever quarter it may arise, in whatever mode it may be communicated, and to whatever consequences it may lead; knowing that the tendency of truth

THE CHARGE.

truth must ever be ultimately beneficial; and to all your researches, you must add earnest prayer to the Father of lights, for wisdom and instruction to guard you from every criminal, from every pernicious error.

I am far from maintaining that by this means you will secure infallibility. I am well apprized of the narrow limits of the human intellect, and the force of inveterate prejudice, often most powerful and most obvious to others, when least perceived or suspected by those who are the subjects of its baneful influence. But this I will assert, that when you have followed the directions which have just been prescribed, you have done all that feeble, fallible human nature will admit. That doctrine which you discover by these means, is to you the pure, unadulterated doctrine of Christ. This doctrine you must teach; without presuming either to conceal it, to add to it, or to take from it. And at the same time that you cannot but regard other systems of opinions as corruptions of christianity, and cannot but think it your duty to warn your hearers against them, so far as they appear to have a pernicious tendency, I am very sure that you will never think of exerting an authority which, with whatever propriety it might be claimed by an apostle who had the gift of discerning spirits, can never, without the greatest indecency, be arrogated by fallible creatures, who have no such pretensions, the authority of anathematizing those whose sentiments differ from your own. If truth is your only object, you will not wish to support your own system of opinions any farther than they are consistent with truth, and by means which will not disgrace your character either as a christian or a gentleman; and you will hold yourself under obligation to the friend who will detect the falshood of any principle which you entertain, how well grounded, how dear, how sacred soever, it may have been esteemed.

Permit

Permit me, Sir, to put the queftion, ftrange as it may found, whether there may not be fome danger of corrupting the word of God, even by the ufe of fcripture language, by the promifcuous introduction of fcripture phrafes, without annexing to them diftinct ideas, or proper explanations. You well know that phrafeology perfectly intelligible in one age and country, is often, by difference of circumftances, and modes of thinking, quite unintelligible in another, and that the bold metaphorical ftyle of the Eaft, is ill adapted to the frigid conceptions, and fober reafonings of the inhabitants of the Weft. But the principal obftruction to a right underftanding of the fcriptures, is, that we all come to the reading of them, prepoffeffed with our own fyftems, and interpret the language of them agreeably to our own hypothefes, without once afking ourfelves the queftion, whether our fyftems be the fame with thofe of the facred writers, or whether they ufed their words in the fenfe
which

which we annex to them. And in fact, it often happens, that the ideas which we have been taught to annex to scripture expressions, are such as never entered into the thoughts of the writers of the New Testament, and that their true meaning, when first discovered, frequently appears cold and far-fetched. From these considerations, I am sure you will infer the necessity of studying the scriptures with the closest attention, and of making them their own interpreters: of expounding them frequently to your hearers so as to lead them into their true meaning, that they may judge of the sense of a passage not merely by the sound of the words, but by the connexion in which they stand, and by the meaning of similar phraseology in corresponding passages. You will also see the necessity of frequently explaining difficult and doubtful phrases which you may occasionally introduce into your public discourses, and which custom and prejudice may lead your hearers to understand in a sense very

different

different from what you apprehend to be the genuine meaning of the scriptures.

I am not afraid, Sir, that you will misapprehend the hints that I have suggested. You will be far from thinking that I intend the slightest disrespect to the sacred oracles. And I am confident that you will agree with me, that the greatest respect is then paid to the scriptures, when they are studied with the closest attention, and explained with the greatest freedom and impartiality.

We are not as many who corrupt the word of God, but as of *sincerity*; this is the second characteristic of the spirit of a christian minister.

By *sincerity* in this connexion, I understand the *undisguised declaration of truth, without regard to personal consequences*. It is such conduct as challenges the severest scrutiny, and will bear the test of the
strongest

ftrongeft and cleareft light, as the original word imports*.

To be fincere, then, is to act upon the beft motives, it is to be open and undifguifed, it is to *declare the whole counfel of God,* and *to keep back nothing profitable* †. It is to teach boldly, and explicitly, whatever appears to be the genuine doctrine of chriftianity. All revealed truth muft be important; an uninterefting unprofitable doctrine of revelation is an abfurdity, it is a contradiction in terms, it is an affront to the perfections of God. To fuppofe that God would reveal a truth, the knowledge and belief of which would be of no ufe to mankind, is to fuppofe that infinite wifdom would act the part of fuperlative folly. And nothing can be more evident, than that a fincere and explicit profeffion of what appears to us to be truth, is the only means by which truth can make its way, and finally pre-

---

* Ειλικρινειας.   † Acts xx. 20. 27.

vail

vail in the world. To conceal what we believe to be the genuine doctrine of revelation under ambiguous expressions, is to betray the sacred trust reposed in us, it is to abandon the divine cause in which we are embarked, it is to be *ashamed of of Christ and of his words.* Not that I mean to disparage christian prudence; far from it. There is such a thing as *casting pearls before swine.* Our divine Master and his apostles, have taught us both by precept and example, to unite the *wisdom of the serpent* with the simplicity and *innocence of the dove,* and to avoid giving unnecessary offence in the discharge of our important embassy. No one will say that it is the duty of a minister to publish every doubt that rises in his mind; much less to puzzle and perplex plain unlettered christians, who come to be instructed in the grand principles of wisdom and virtue, with subtle controversies upon intricate and difficult questions. But in all points of importance, where his own mind is quite satisfied, surely it is a minister's duty to speak out boldly, and where he is in

suspence,

suspence, sincerity will not permit him to express himself with confidence. Prudence must judge in all. But let not christian prudence degenerate into worldly wisdom. Of this there is the utmost danger. To temporize and to disguise unpopular opinions, to flatter men in ignorance and prejudice, is the way to ease, to affluence, and to applause. But to be honest and sincere, to speak truth without disguise, and to oppose established errors, often leads to poverty, reproach, desertion, and contempt. Judge then, upon which side the danger lies. Few, I believe, have ever repented being too sincere. Many have been stung with remorse under the consciousness of duplicity of character, and of having, through fear of personal consequences, concealed truth under an ambiguous phraseology. And the cause of truth hath often suffered by the timidity of its professed advocates.

For who, Sir, should be willing to suffer in defence of truth, if the ministers of the gospel are not? How can

we

we expect that our hearers will believe that we are in earnest, if we do not act with the most undisguised simplicity, and are not willing to take the consequences of avowing important truth? It is by the sufferings of its advocates and champions, that the wisdom of providence hath ordained that truth shall make its way. Our divine master was the first to fall in the glorious struggle. His apostles and their disciples followed his great example, and sealed their testimony with their blood. The reformers of the church from the corruptions of popery, were animated by the same spirit of christian heroism. And in the present age of comparative toleration, if we would approve ourselves the genuine disciples and faithful ministers of Christ, we must be content to bear his cross, we must be willing at the command of providence, to *forsake all and follow him*; and must *account the reproach of Christ greater riches than the treasures of the earth.*

My

My earnest advice therefore is, Be prudent; do not give unnecessary offence. Do not expose yourself to unnecessary hazard and inconvenience. Do not unnecessarily impede your acceptance and usefulness. But above all, *Be honest and sincere.* Secure to yourself the broad impenetrable shield of a good conscience. Keep *back nothing that is profitable. Handle not the word of God deceitfully.* And, as you will answer for your sacred trust another day, suffer no consideration of ease, reputation, or interest, to move you to betray the high cause in which you are embarked. *Let this be your rejoicing, even the testimony of your conscience, that in simplicity and godly sincerity, not with fleshly wisdom, but by the grace of God you have your conversation in the world.*

The apostle mentions another characteristic of a christian minister, which is, to *speak and act as in the sight of* God.

And

And O! what will be the temper and conduct of that minister who sets God always before him; who in every action of his life and ministry, doth, as it were, behold the eye of the supreme Being fixed steadily and invariably upon him for purposes the most interesting, the most awful, and the most encouraging; to pity, to guide, and to succour under every difficulty; to aid every generous exertion, and to mark, and frown upon, every wilful neglect of duty. Under such impressions, with what earnest solicitude will a minister prepare for the duties of his office, that he may not in the sight of God speak, or do, any thing unworthy of his character, that he may not offer the sacrifice of fools, nor utter crude and indigested ramblings in the name, and in the presence of God! With what plainness and freedom, with what fortitude, with what dignity and energy, with what infinite superiority to mean and secular views, with what indifference to human applause, with what unconcern as to personal consequences, will he declare *the whole counsel of God*; not daring to conceal what he believes to be important, that so he may be *clear of the blood of all men!* With what diligence will he seek, with what eagerness will he embrace, every opportunity of promoting the great ends of his ministry, instructing the ignorant, reclaiming the vicious, recovering the wanderer to the paths of wisdom and virtue, administering consolation to the afflicted, confirming and establishing the sincere christian! How will the apprehension of the divine inspection rouse him to unremitting exertions, whatever difficulties he may meet with, whatever temptations to negligence and supineness, with whatever indifference and neglect his services may be treated, whatever ungrateful treatment he may receive, or how little soever his apparent success may be! And what a tendency will this persuasion have, to engage the christian minister often to lift up his heart in devout aspirations after a divine assistance and blessing, and to ascribe

ascribe all that is good in himself, and all the success of his ministry, to the favour of the Almighty. Rejoicing in the consciousness of having laboured faithfully, abundantly, and successfully, he will humbly and thankfully add, *yet not I, but the grace of God which was with me.*

I cannot then, Sir, conclude with a better advice or wish, than this, that you would *set the Lord always before you,* and that in the whole course of your ministry, you would *study to approve yourself to God,* to glorify his name, and to accomplish his will.

And permit me to add for your encouragement, that with this temper, and with these views your final success is infallible. If the object of your ministry be interest or applause, you may very possibly miss your aim; and if attained, how worthless, how contemptible an end! But if you have no other view than to be approved of God, and to accomplish his will,

will, you cannot be difappointed in your purpofe. It is hard to fuppofe that vigorous exertions upon fuch generous principles can fail of being eminently ufeful. But if the fupreme Arbiter of events do not fee fit to employ you as an inftrument in promoting the caufe of truth and virtue in the world (and who fhall prefume to dictate to him?) he can bow your will in placid refignation to his fovereign pleafure. And in the mean time, the generous purpofe of the willing mind, with which he is perfectly acquainted, will in his account, be entered in your favour, as though it had been actually accomplifhed; and in the great day of final remuneration, it will not be forgotten that you had *it in your heart to have built a houfe to his name.*

THE END.

www.ingramcontent.com/pod-product-compliance
Lightning Source LLC
Chambersburg PA
CBHW030250170426
43202CB00009B/695